Non-verbal Reasoning

Assessment Papers

Stretch

9–10 years

UNIVERSITY PRESS

Great Clarendon Street, Oxford, OX2 6DP, United Kingdom

Oxford University Press is a department of the University of Oxford.
It furthers the University's objective of excellence in research,
scholarship, and education by publishing worldwide. Oxford is
a registered trade mark of Oxford University Press in the UK and in
certain other countries

British Library Cataloguing in Publication Data
Data available

978-0-19-274213-1

10 9 8 7 6 5

Paper used in the production of this book is a natural, recyclable
product made from wood grown in sustainable forests.
The manufacturing process conforms to the environmental
regulations of the country of origin.

Printed in China

Acknowledgements

The publishers would like to thank the following for permissions to
use copyright material:

Page make-up: eMC Design Ltd
Illustrations: OKS Group
Cover illustrations: Lo Cole

Although we have made every effort to trace and contact all
copyright holders before publication this has not been possible in all
cases. If notified, the publisher will rectify any errors or omissions at
the earliest opportunity.

Links to third party websites are provided by Oxford in good faith
and for information only. Oxford disclaims any responsibility for
the materials contained in any third party website referenced in
this work.

What is Bond?

The Bond *Stretch* series is a new addition to the Bond range of assessment papers, the number one series for the 11$^+$, selective exams and general practice. Bond *Stretch* is carefully designed to challenge above and beyond the level provided in the regular Bond assessment range.

How does this book work?

The book contains two distinct sets of papers, along with full answers and a Progress Chart.

- Focus tests, accompanied by advice and directions, are focused on particular (and age-appropriate) non-verbal reasoning question types encountered in the 11$^+$ and other exams, but devised at a higher level than the standard *Assessment Papers*. Each Focus test is designed to help raise a child's skills in the question type, as well as offer plenty of practice for the necessary techniques.

- Mixed papers are full-length tests containing a full range of non-verbal reasoning question types. These are designed to provide rigorous practice for children working at a level higher than that required to pass at the 11$^+$ and other non-verbal reasoning tests.

Full answers are provided for both types of test in the middle of the book.

How much time should the tests take?

The tests are for practice and to reinforce learning, and you may wish to test exam techniques and working to a set time limit. Using the Mixed papers, we would recommend your child spends 30 minutes answering the 48 questions in each paper.

You can reduce the suggested time by five minutes to practise working at speed.

Using the Progress Chart

The Progress Chart can be used to track Focus test and Mixed paper results over time to monitor how well your child is doing and identify any repeated problems in tackling the different question types.

Focus test 1 Similarities

Which of the shapes belongs to the group on the left? Circle the letter.

Example

a b c d e

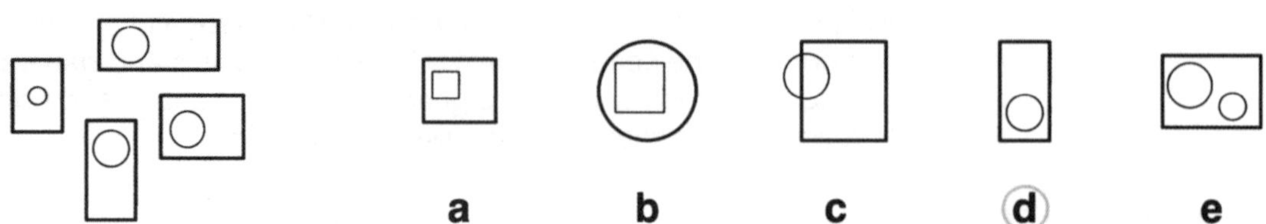

Always look very carefully at the shapes on the left – you often have to notice several things about them, such as shape, shading and position.

1

a b c d e

2

a b c d e

3

a b c d e

4

a b c d e

5

a b c d e

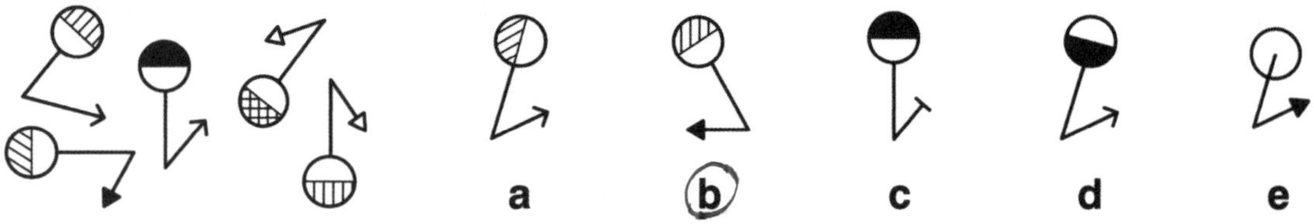

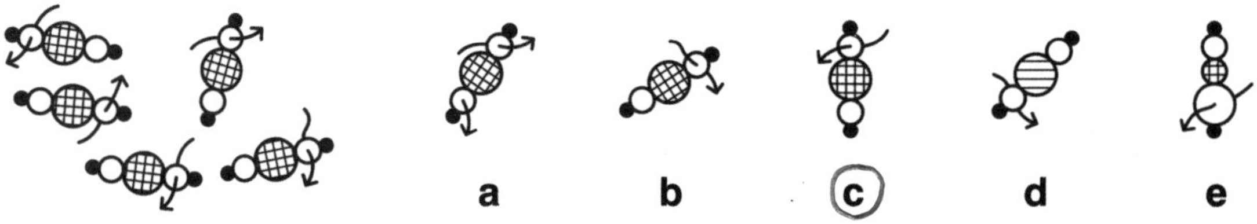

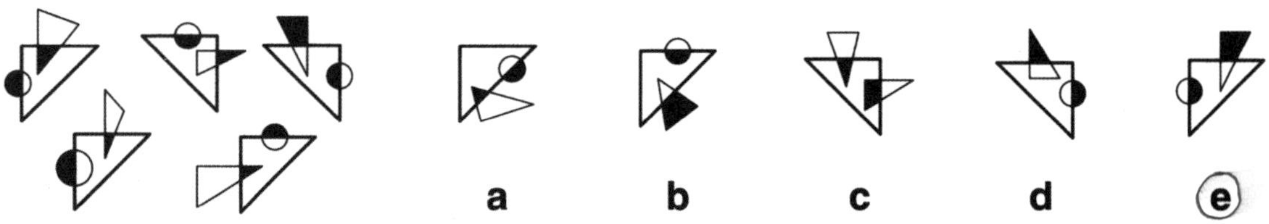

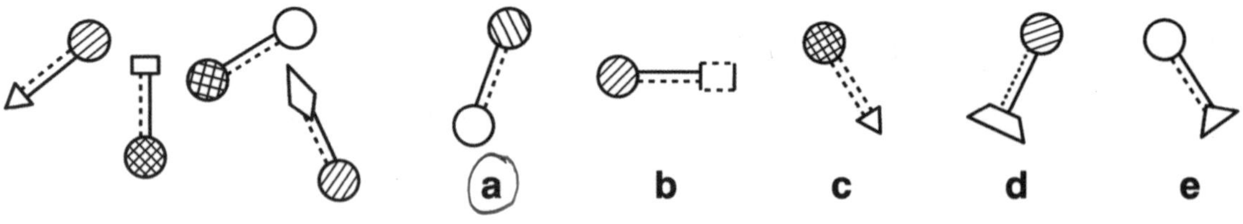

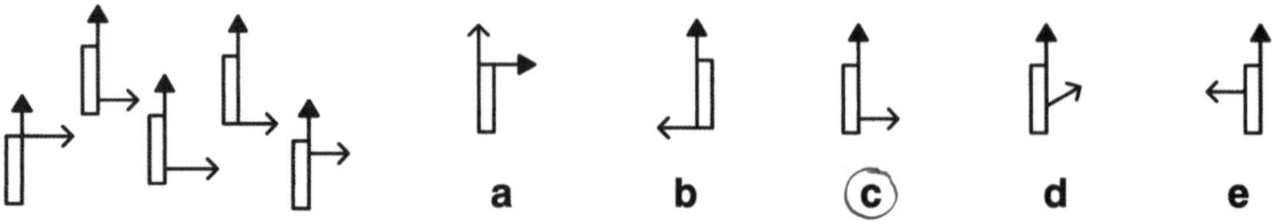

6

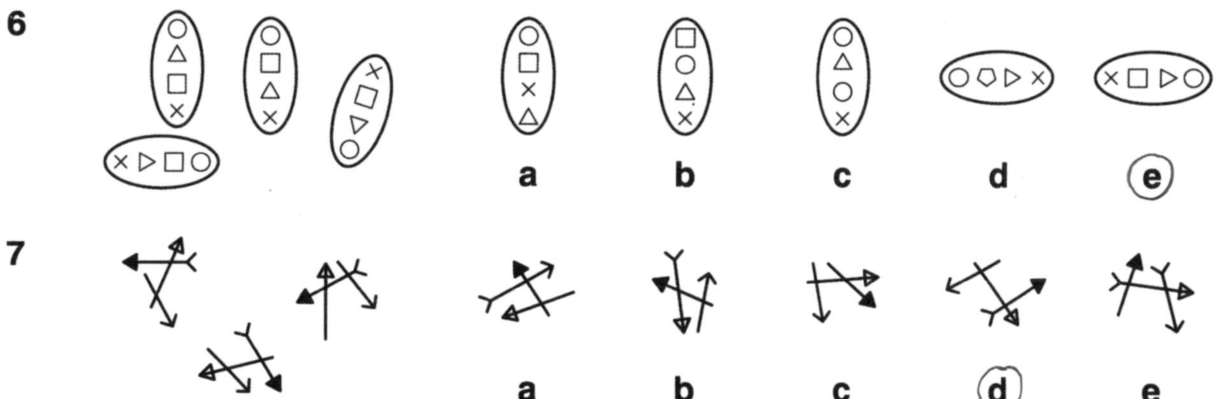

a   b   c   d   **(e)**

7

a   b   c   **(d)**   e

There may be parts of each shape that are not linked together and not part of the information needed to answer the question – spot them, then ignore them!

8

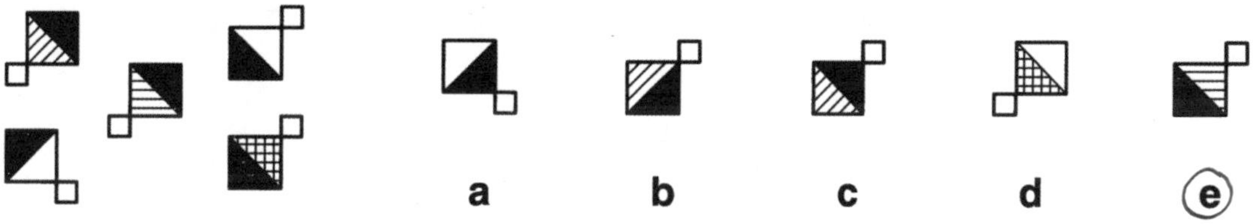

a   b   c   d   **(e)**

9

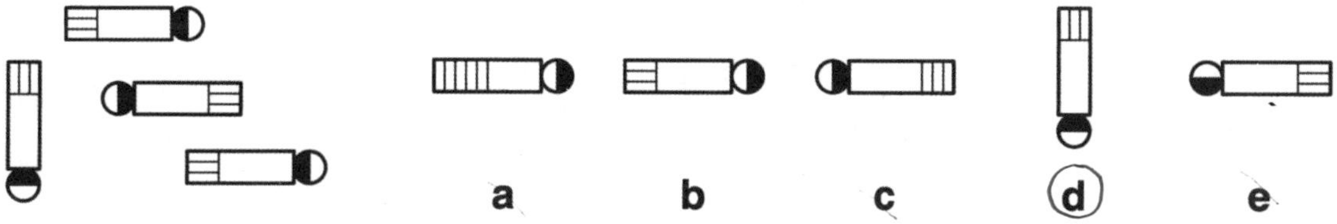

a   b   c   **(d)**   e

10

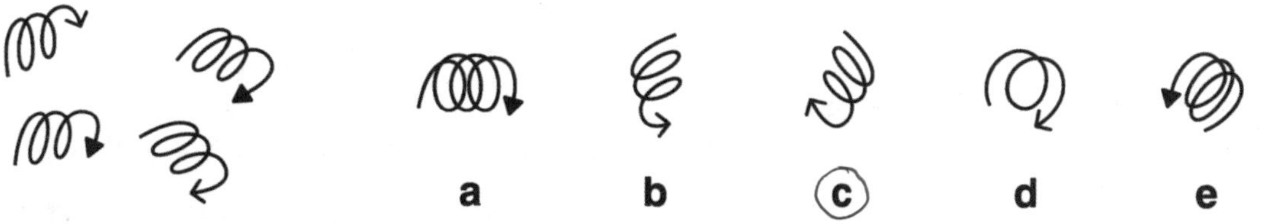

a   b   **(c)**   d   e

11

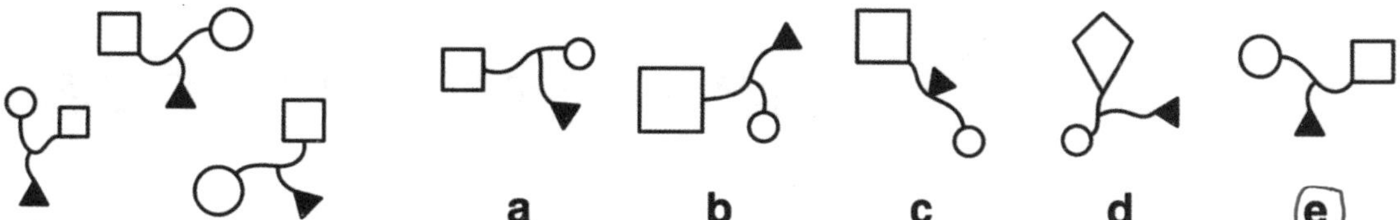

a   b   c   d   **(e)**

12

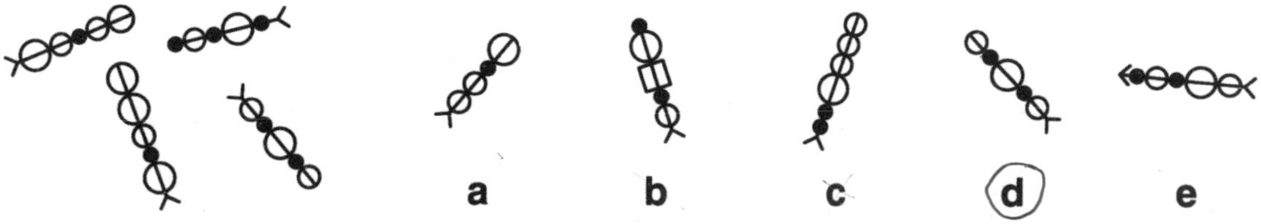

a   b   c   **(d)**   e

Focus test 2 Analogies

Which shape or pattern completes the second pair in the same way as the first pair? Circle the letter.

Example

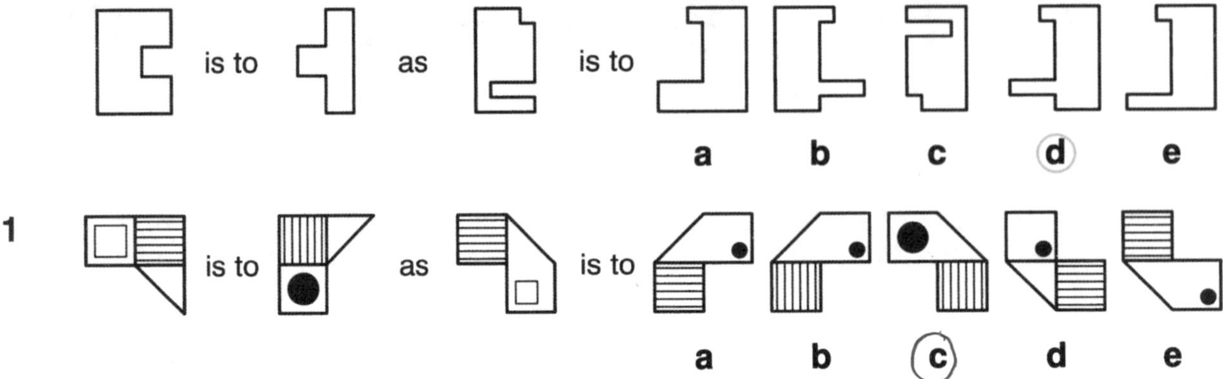

Shapes may be rotated but not 'turned over' – as if they were a jigsaw piece.

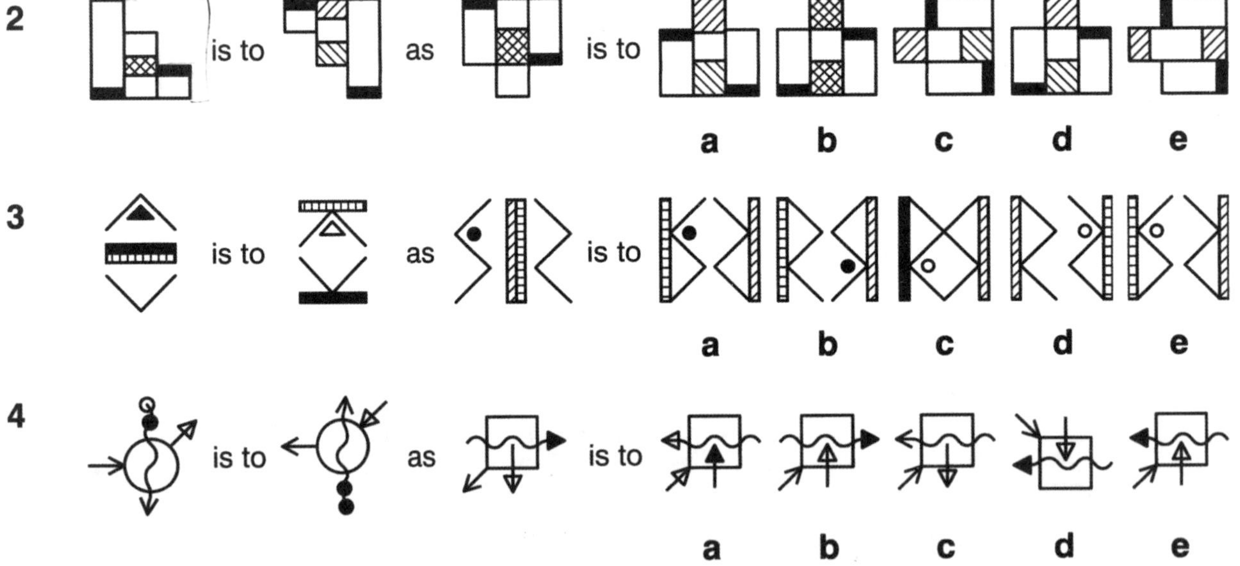

In the next questions, number may be important for parts of a pattern, or for the total number of elements in a pattern.

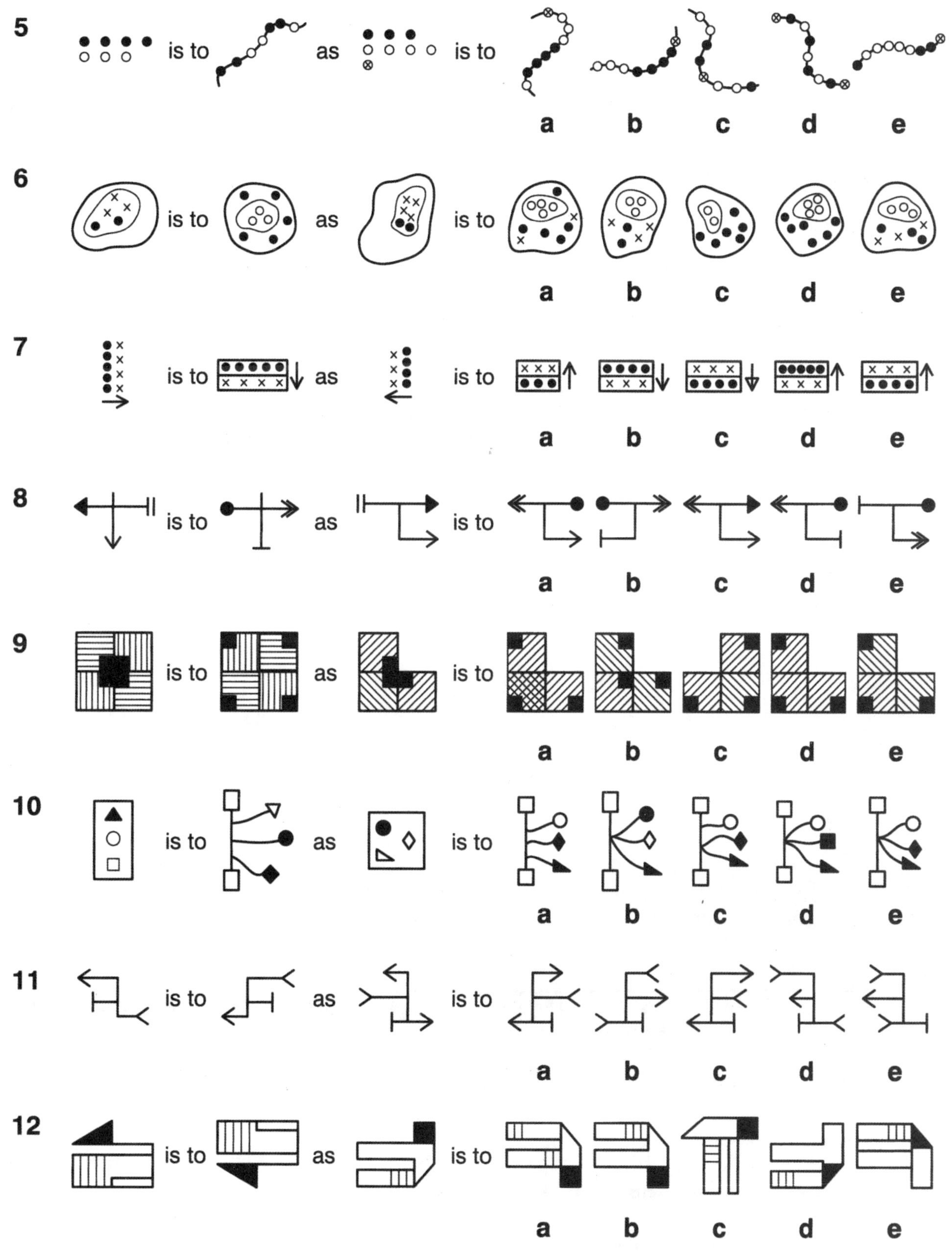

5
is to
as
is to
a b c d e

6
is to
as
is to
a b c d e

7
is to
as
is to
a b c d e

8
is to
as
is to
a b c d e

9
is to
as
is to
a b c d e

10
is to
as
is to
a b c d e

11
is to
as
is to
a b c d e

12
is to
as
is to
a b c d e

Using the given patterns and codes, work out the code that matches the last pattern. Circle the letter.

Example

> Remember, the letters that are in the same position within a code all apply to the same feature, for example, the first letter might be number of sides, the second letter might be shading.

1

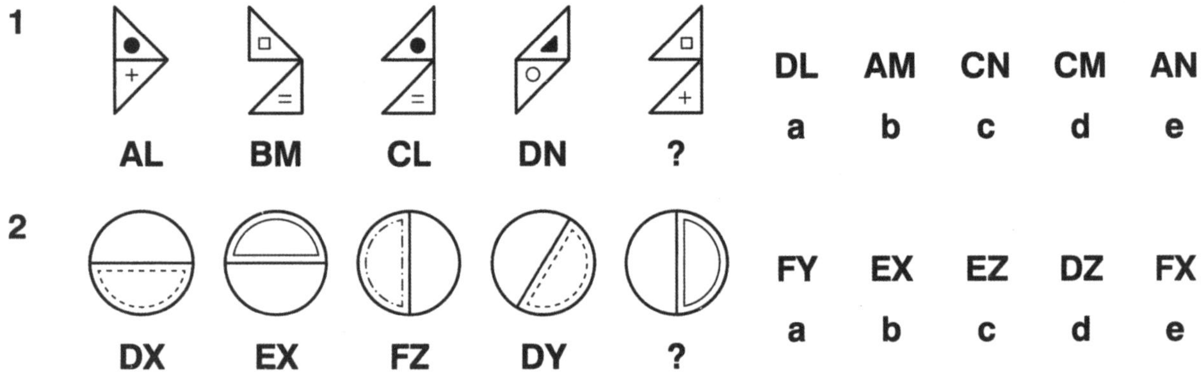

2

> Sometimes, a new variation of a feature may appear in the shape at the end – if so, a new letter will appear in the code options.

3

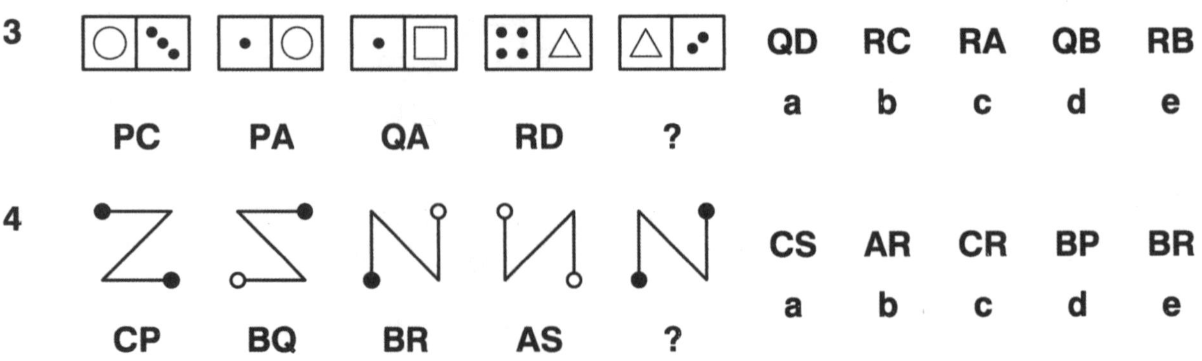

4

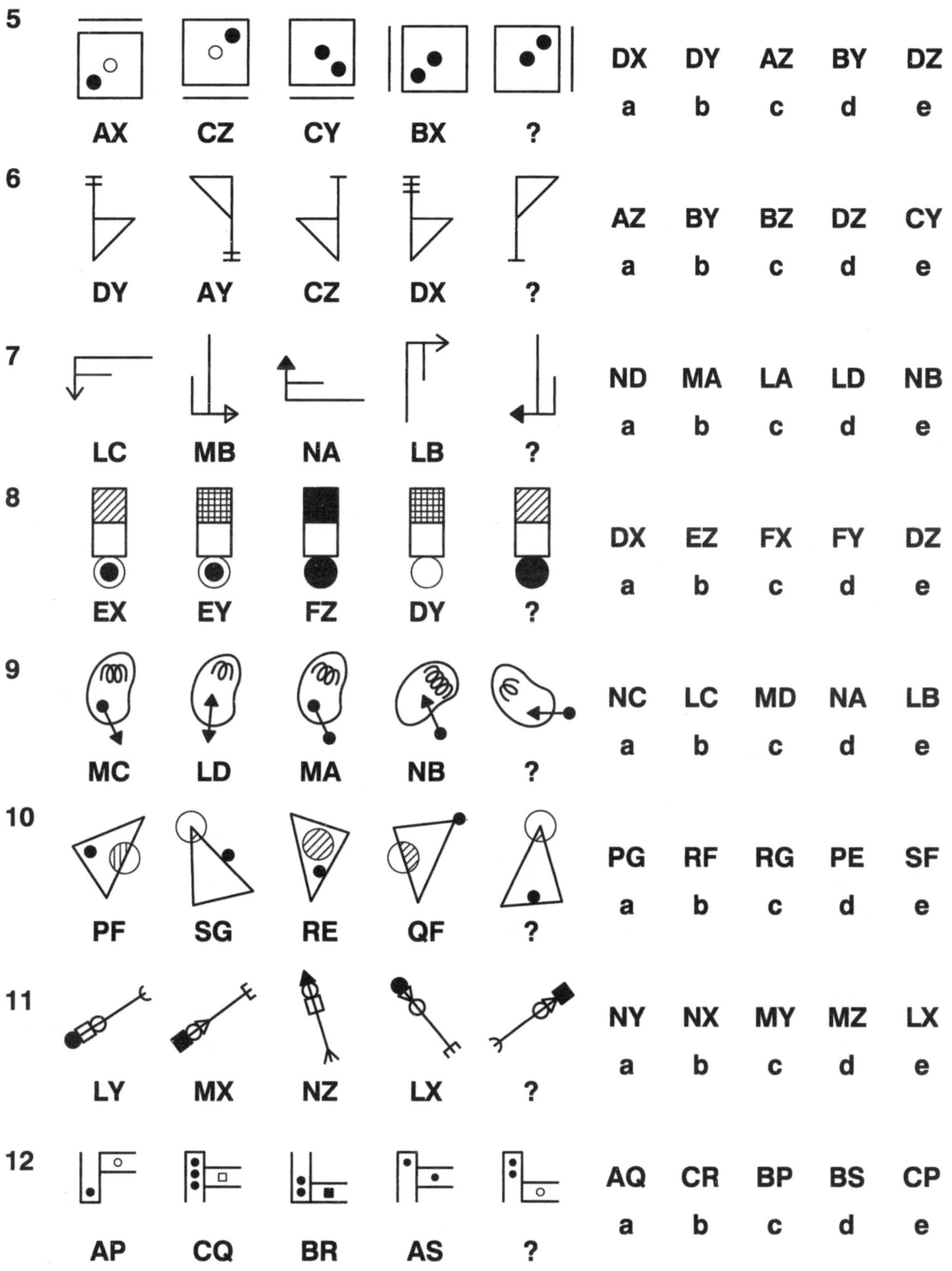

Focus test 4 — Cubes

Which cube could not be made from the given net? Circle the letter.

Example

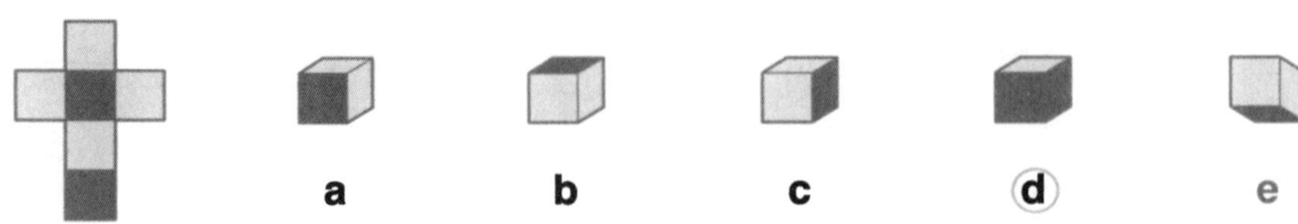

a   b   c   (d)   e

> It is often helpful to start by identifying which 'faces' in the net cannot end up being next to each other in the cube.

1   a   b   c   d   e

2   a   b   c   d   e

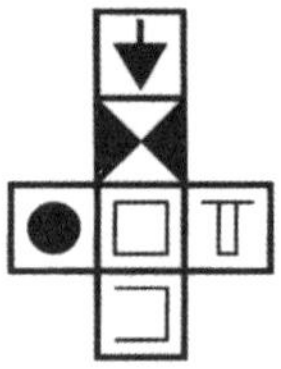

3   a   b   c   d   e

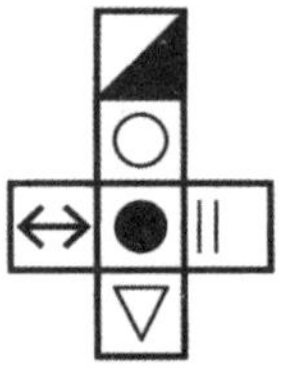

4   a   b   c   d   e

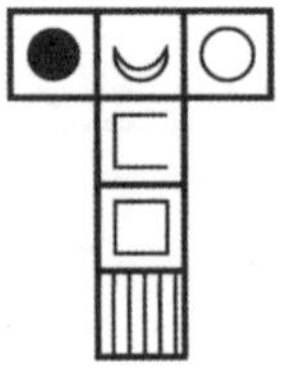

5   a   b   c   d   e

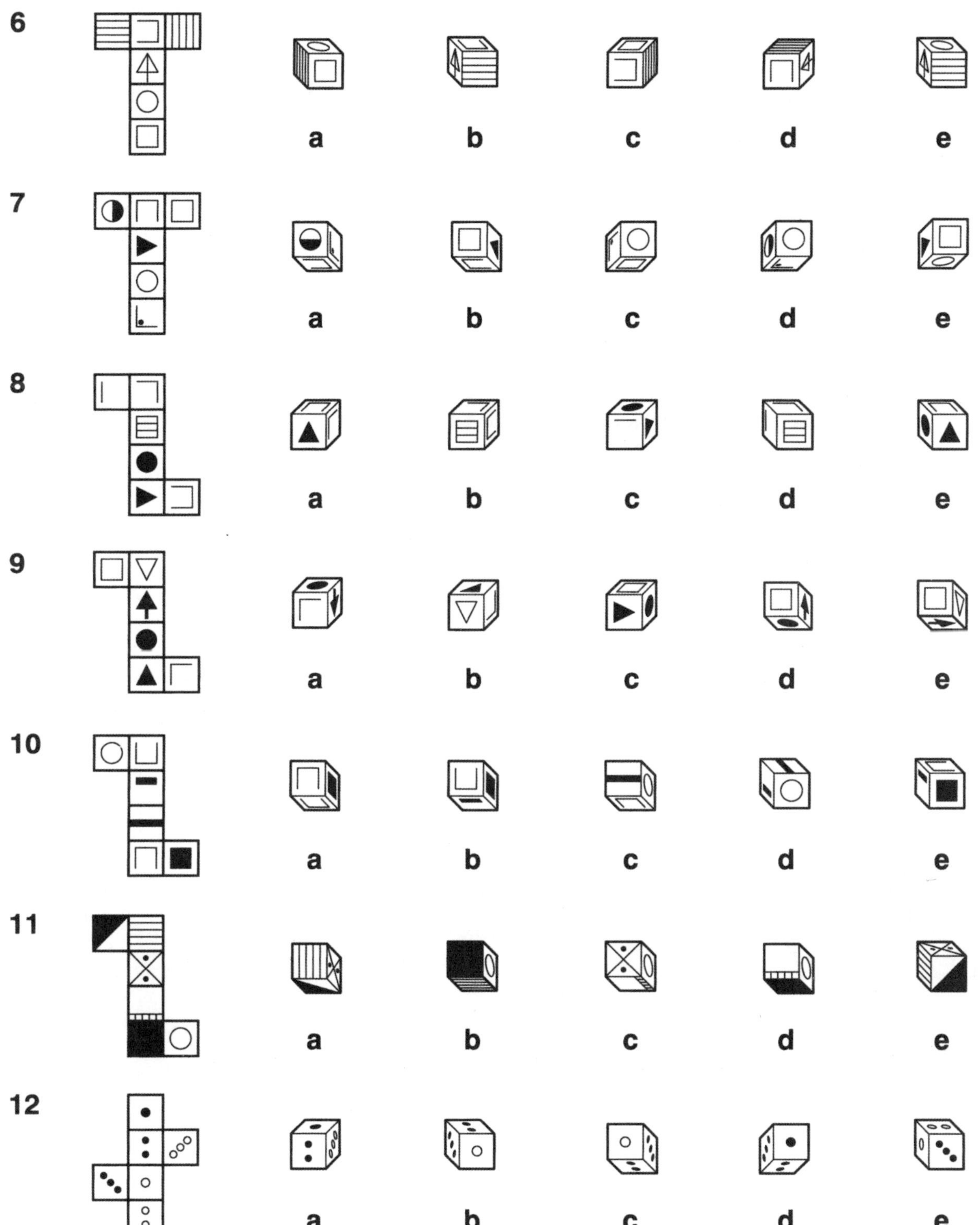

6   a   b   c   d   e

7   a   b   c   d   e

8   a   b   c   d   e

9   a   b   c   d   e

10   a   b   c   d   e

11   a   b   c   d   e

12   a   b   c   d   e

Reflections

Which shape or pattern is a reflection of the shape on the left? Circle the letter.

Example

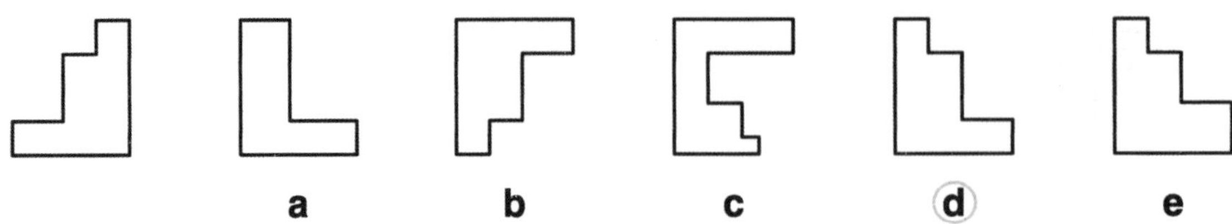

a   b   c   (d)   e

Remember that the line of reflection, or 'mirror line', may be vertical or horizontal.

1   a   b   c   d   e

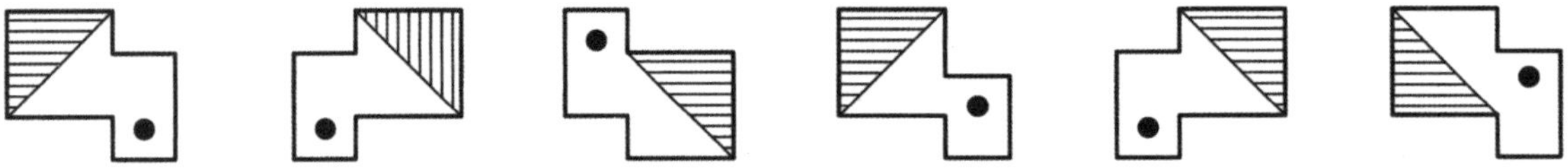

2   a   b   c   d   e

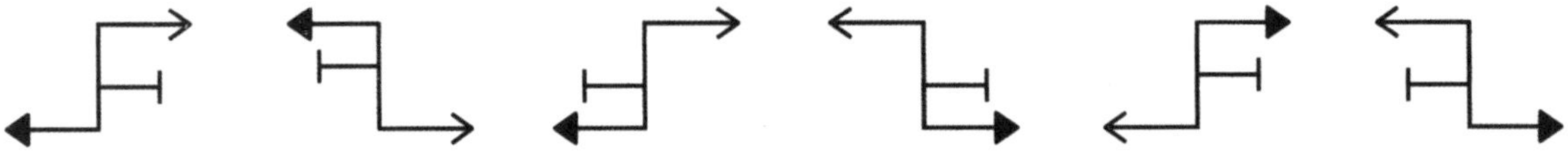

3   a   b   c   d   e

4   a   b   c   d   e

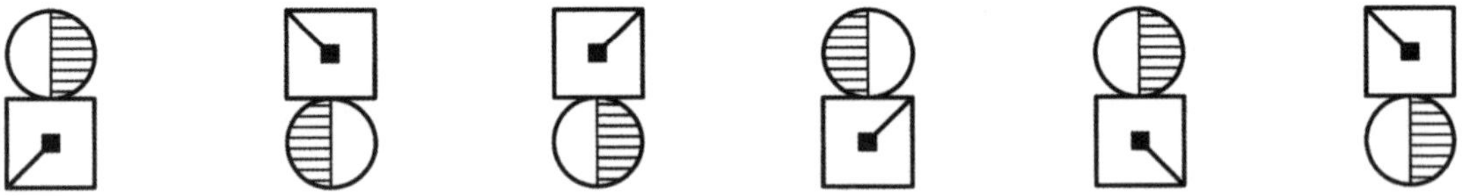

5   a   Reflections   c   d   e

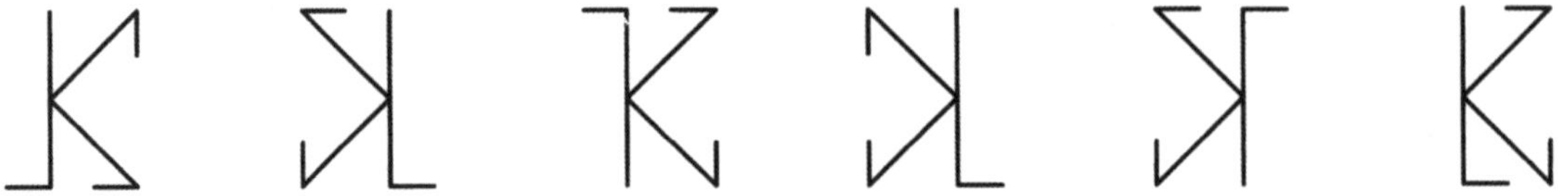

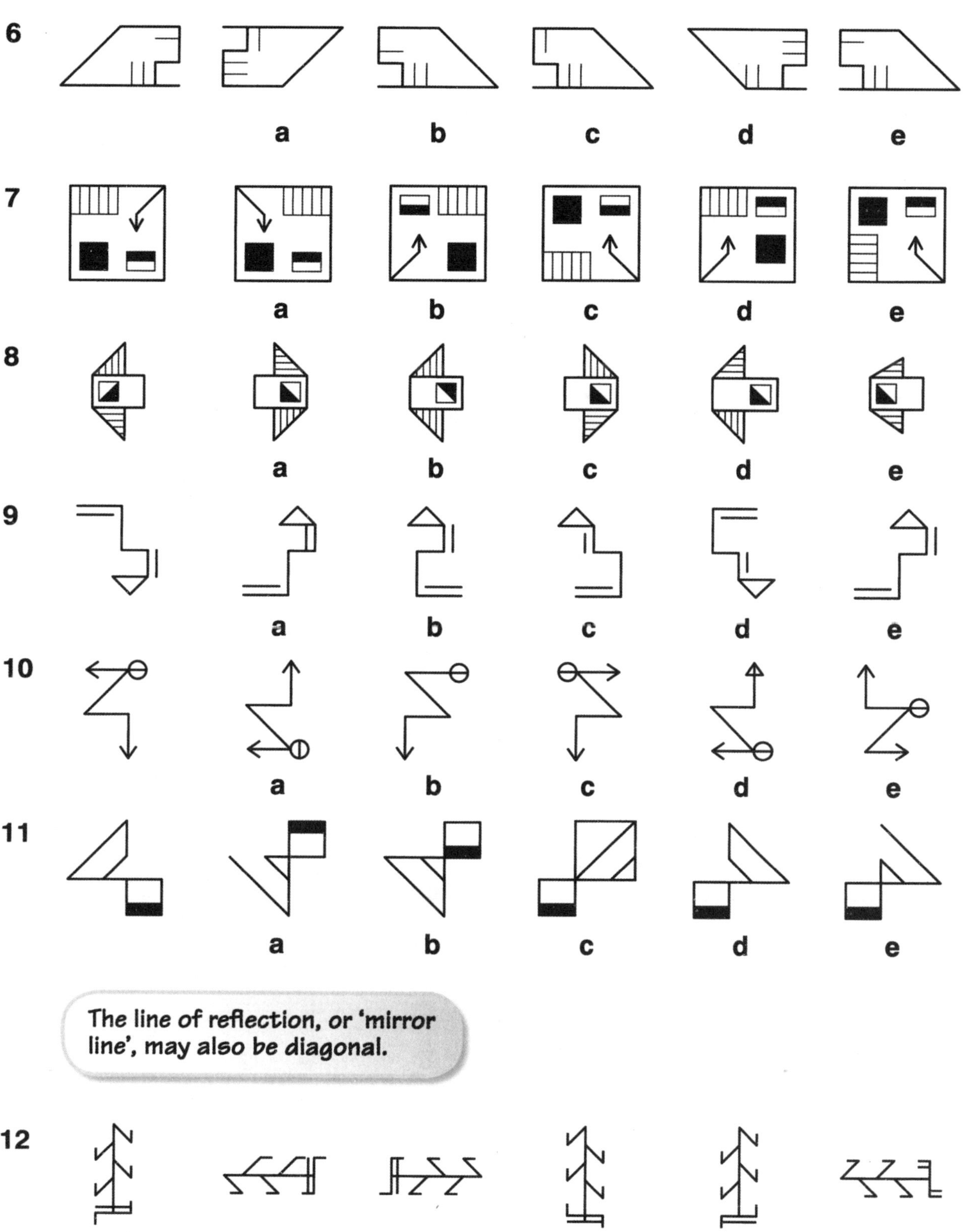

6

     a   **b**   **c**   **d**   **e**

7

     a   **b**   **c**   **d**   **e**

8

     a   **b**   **c**   **d**   **e**

9

     a   **b**   **c**   **d**   **e**

10

     a   **b**   **c**   **d**   **e**

11

     a   **b**   **c**   **d**   **e**

> The line of reflection, or 'mirror line', may also be diagonal.

12

     a   **b**   **c**   **d**   **e**

Sequences

Which shape or pattern continues or completes the given sequence?
Circle the letter.

Example

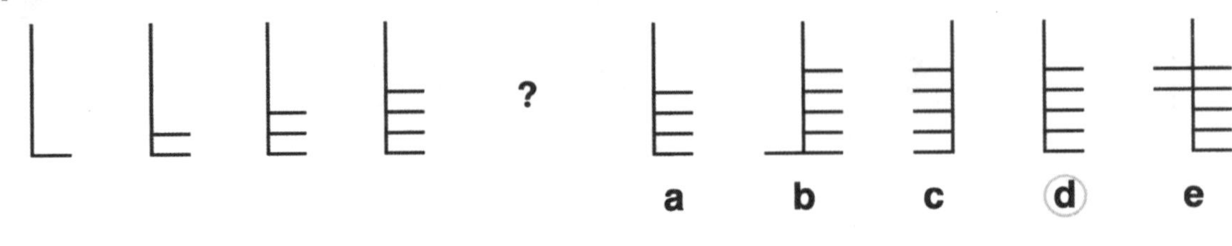

1

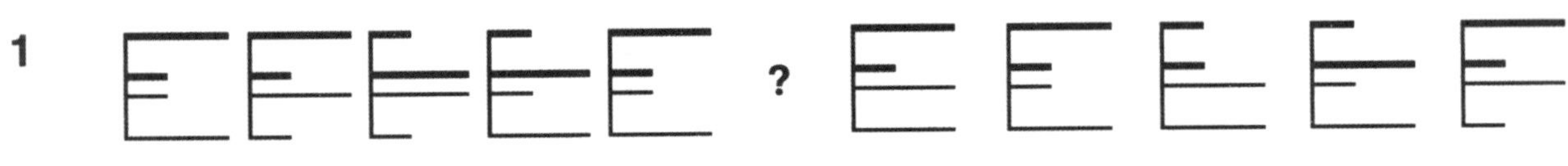

2

Look out for increasing, decreasing and/or alternating patterns within each sequence.

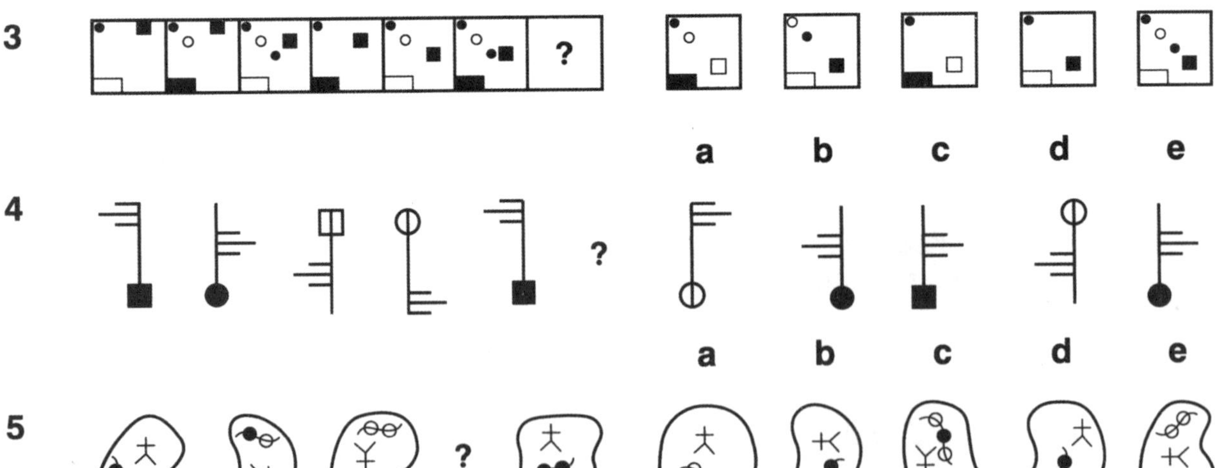

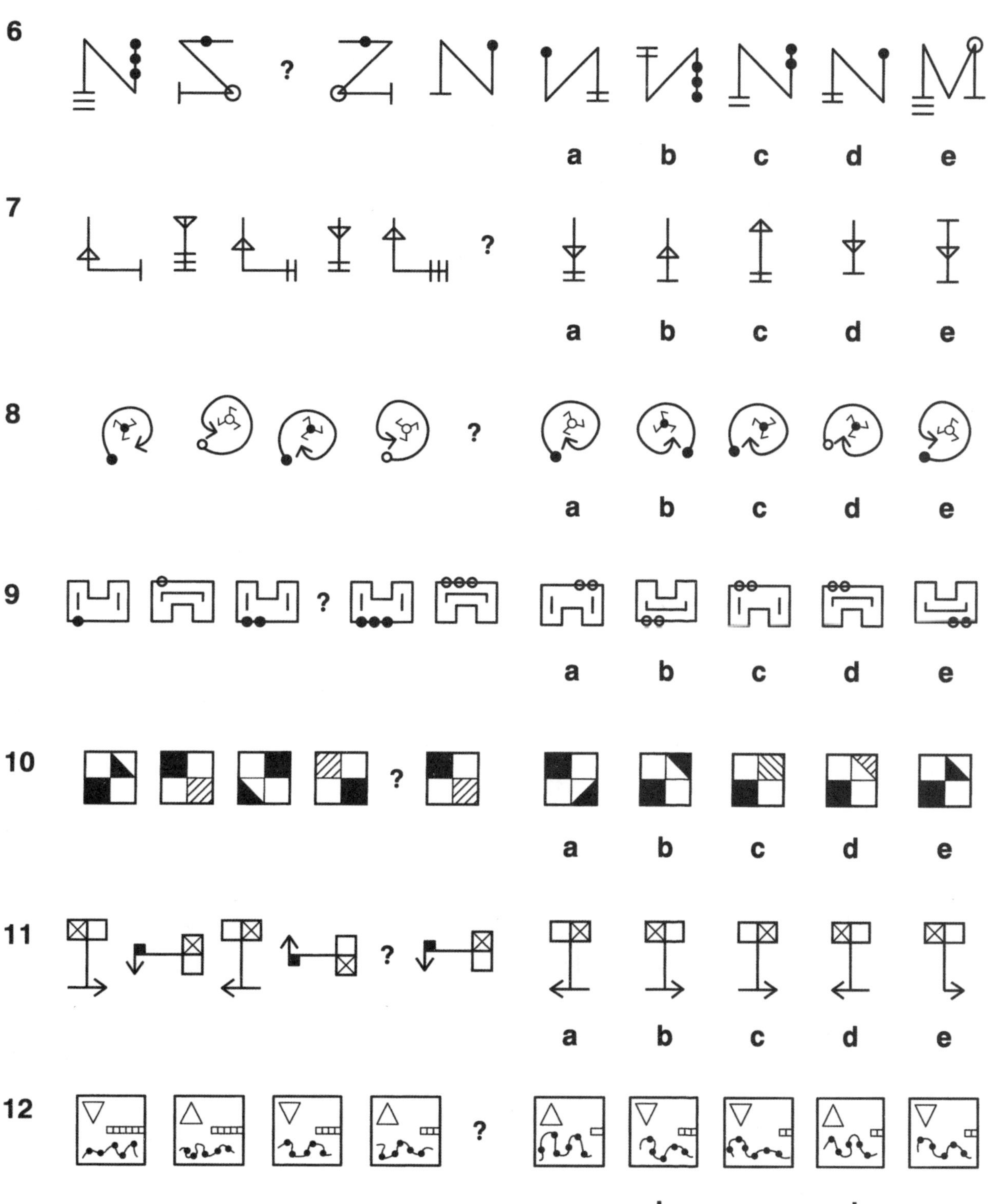

6
a b c d e

7
a b c d e

8
a b c d e

9
a b c d e

10
a b c d e

11
a b c d e

12
a b c d e

Focus test 7   Grids

Which shape or pattern completes the grid on the left? Circle the letter.

Example

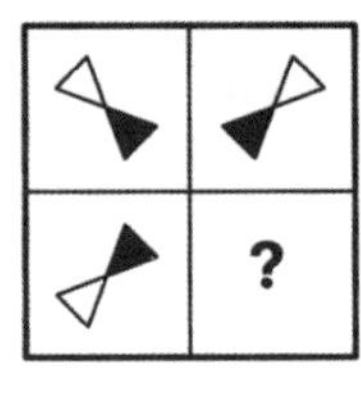

a   b   c   d   e

The whole grid may have a symmetrical pattern ...

1

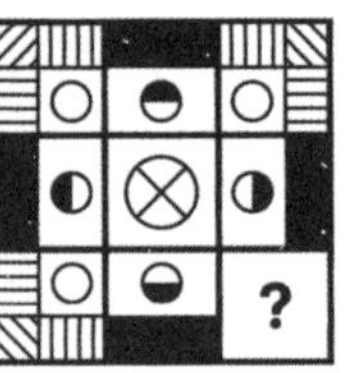

a   b   c   d   e

... or a pattern in the rows ...

2

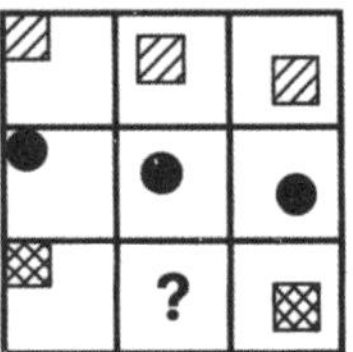

a   b   c   d   e

... or a pattern in the columns.

3

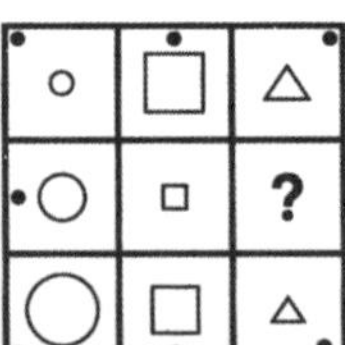

a   b   c   d   e

4

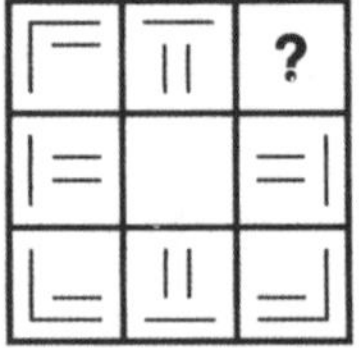

a   b   c   d   e

Sometimes a pattern in the middle is broken up into its separate parts in the surrounding shapes – look carefully at the sections given in the next questions to identify the missing part.

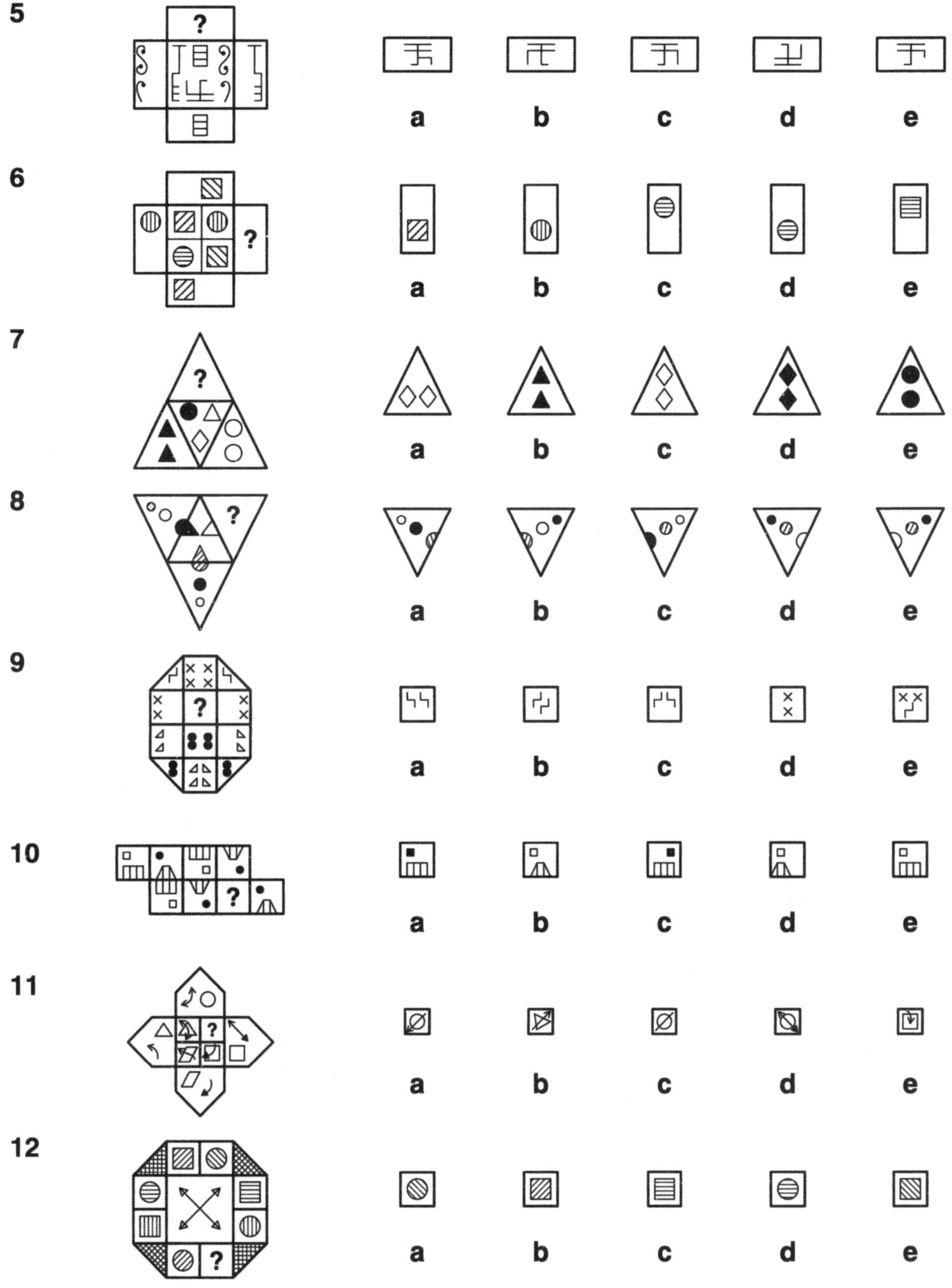

Combining shapes

Which pattern on the right is formed by combining the two shapes on the left? Circle the letter.

Example

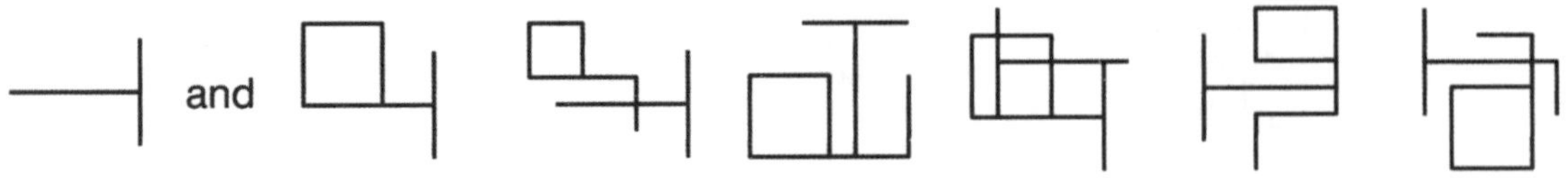

a   b   **c**   d   e

1

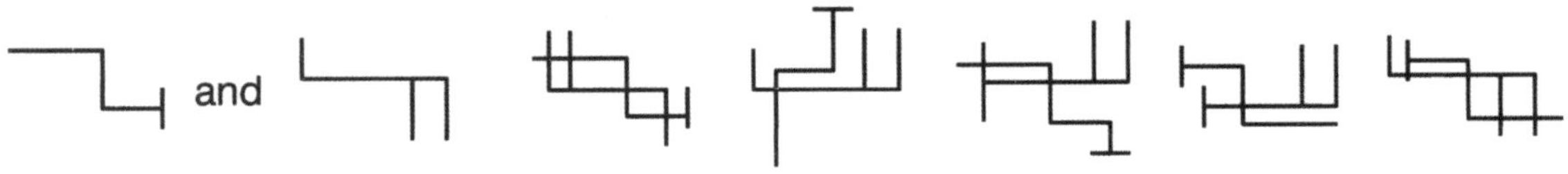

a   b   c   d   e

2

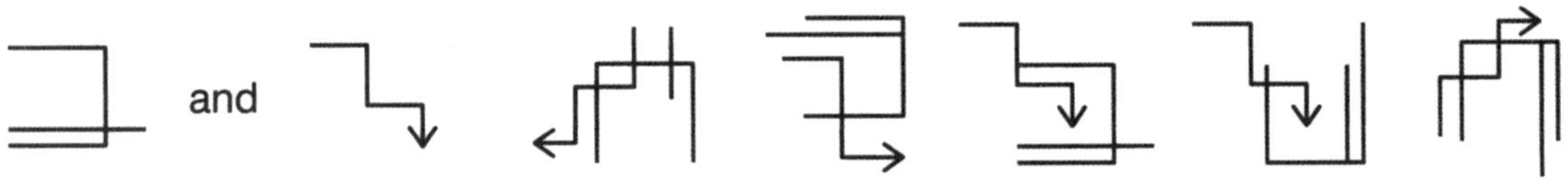

a   b   c   d   e

3

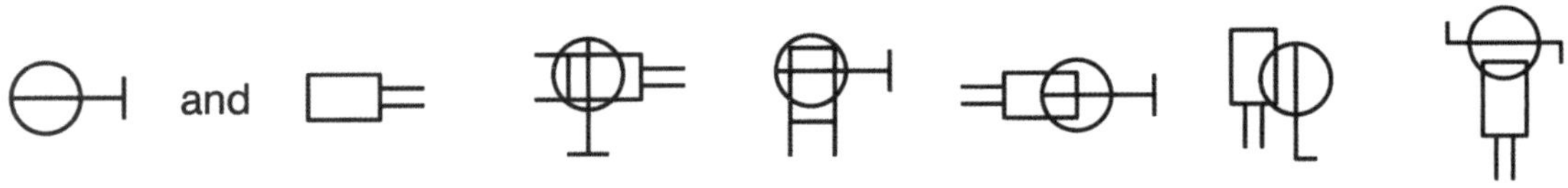

a   b   c   d   e

Remember, shapes may be rotated but not turned over!

4

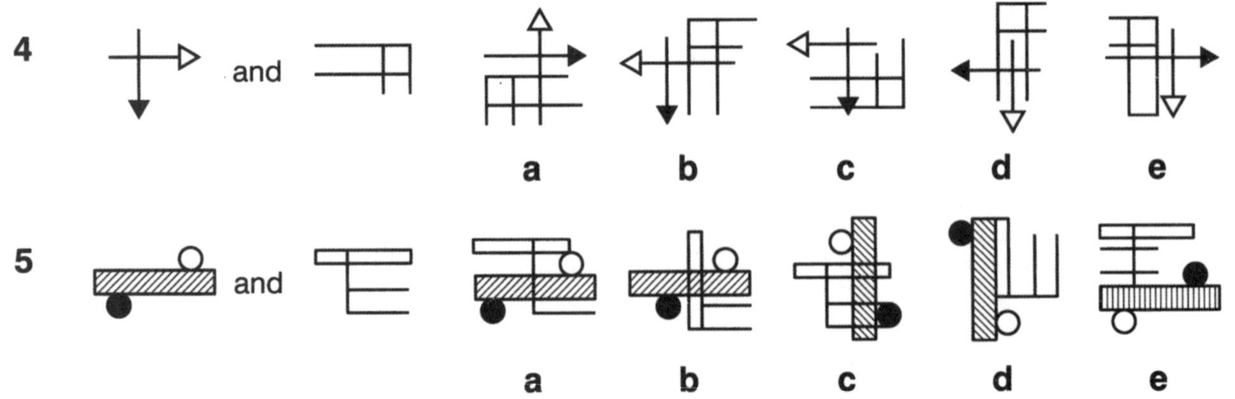

a   b   c   d   e

5

a   b   c   d   e

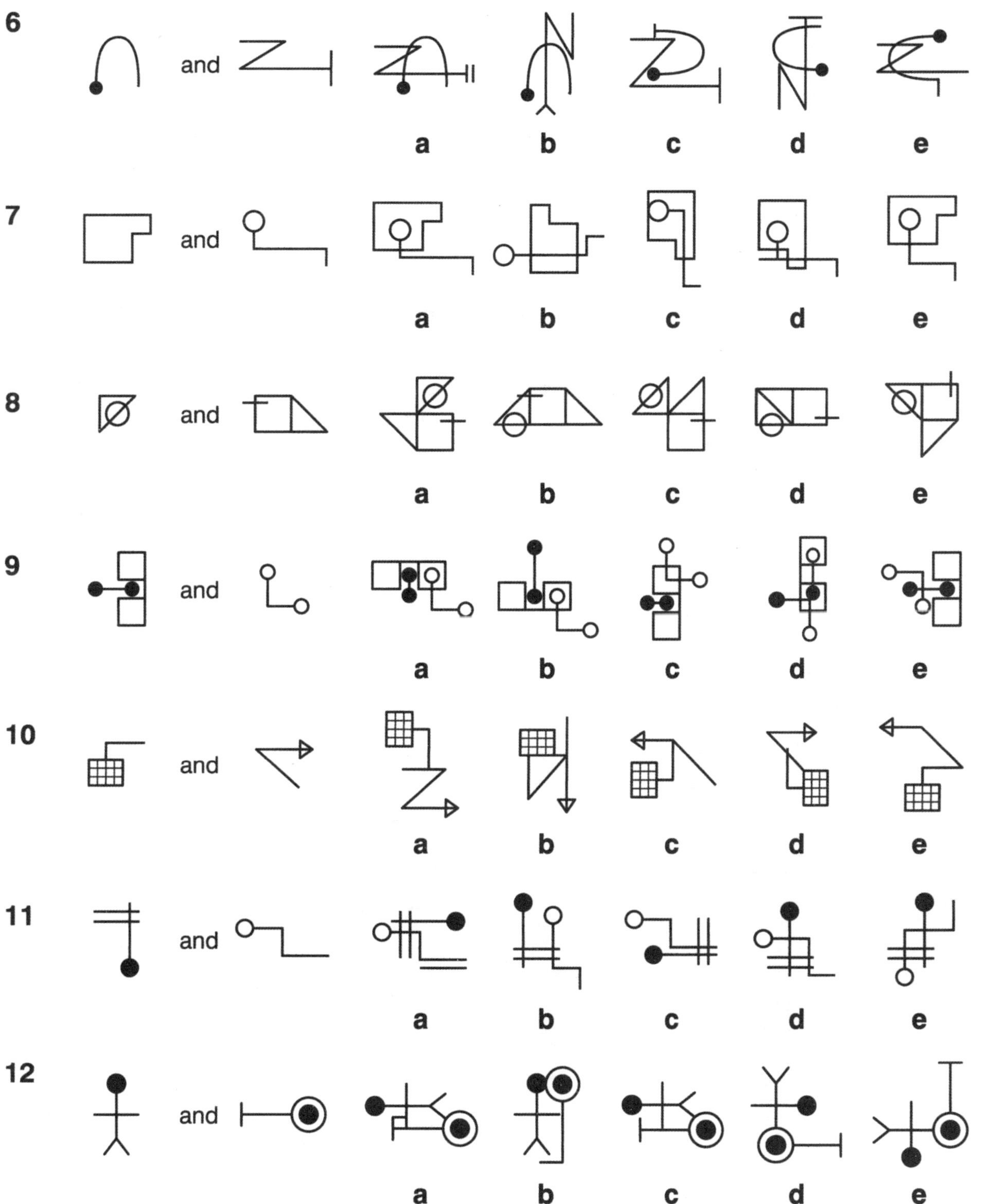

6
and
a
b
c
d
e

7
and
a
b
c
d
e

8
and
a
b
c
d
e

9
and
a
b
c
d
e

10
and
a
b
c
d
e

11
and
a
b
c
d
e

12
and
a
b
c
d
e

Which of the shapes belongs to the group on the left? Circle the letter.

Example

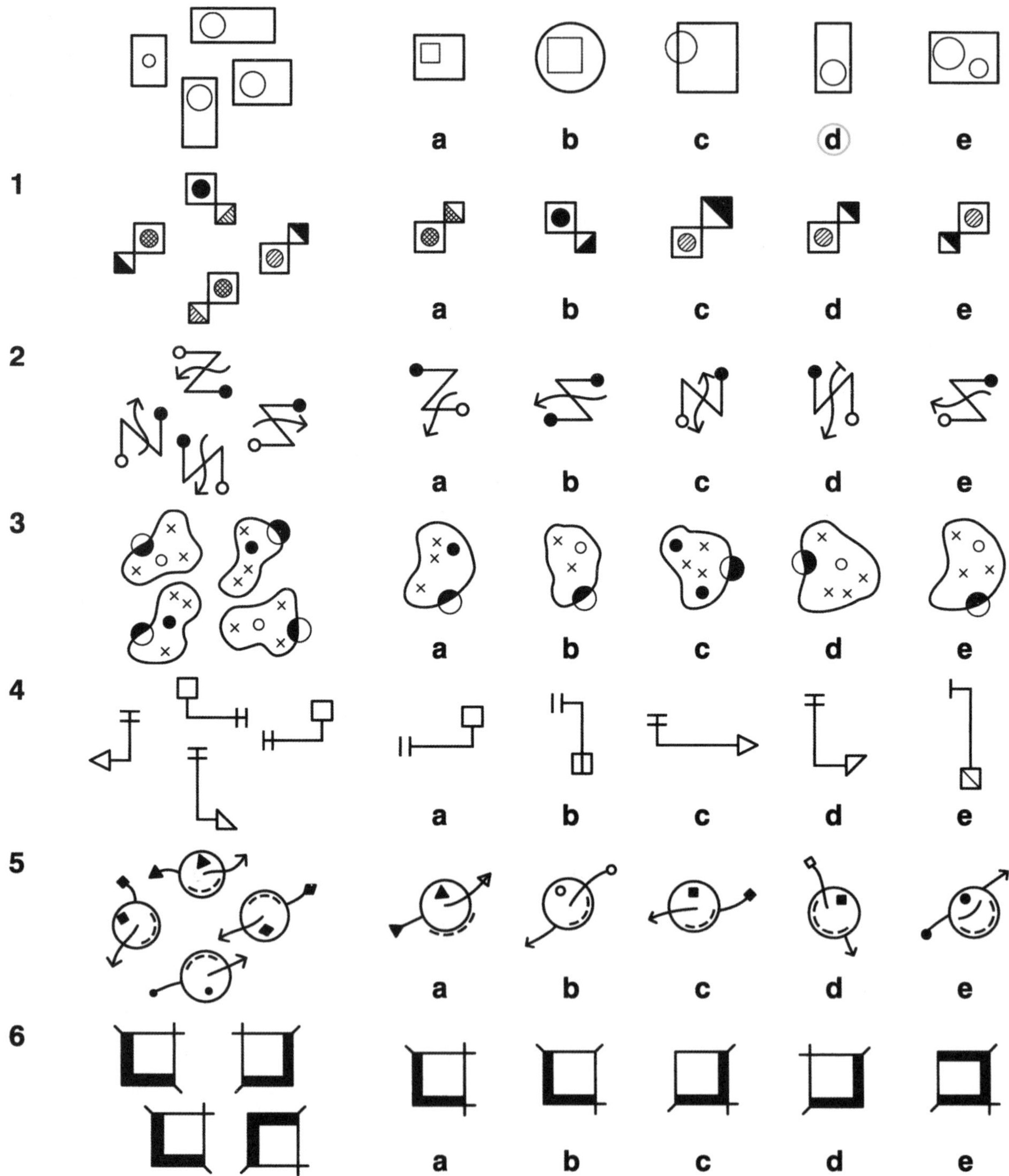

Which shape or pattern completes the second pair in the same way as the first pair? Circle the letter.

Example

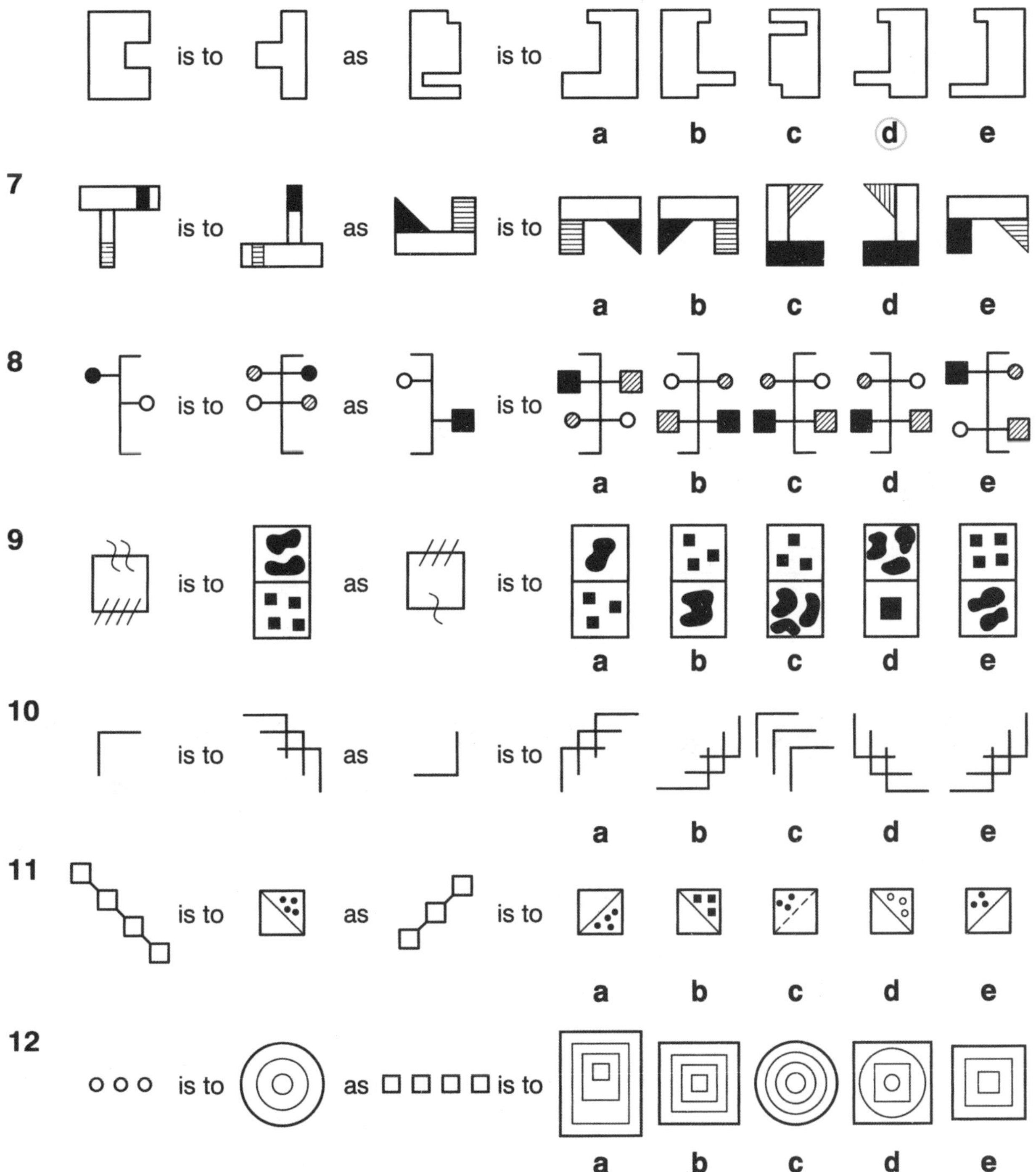

Using the given patterns and codes, work out the code that matches the last pattern. Circle the letter.

Example

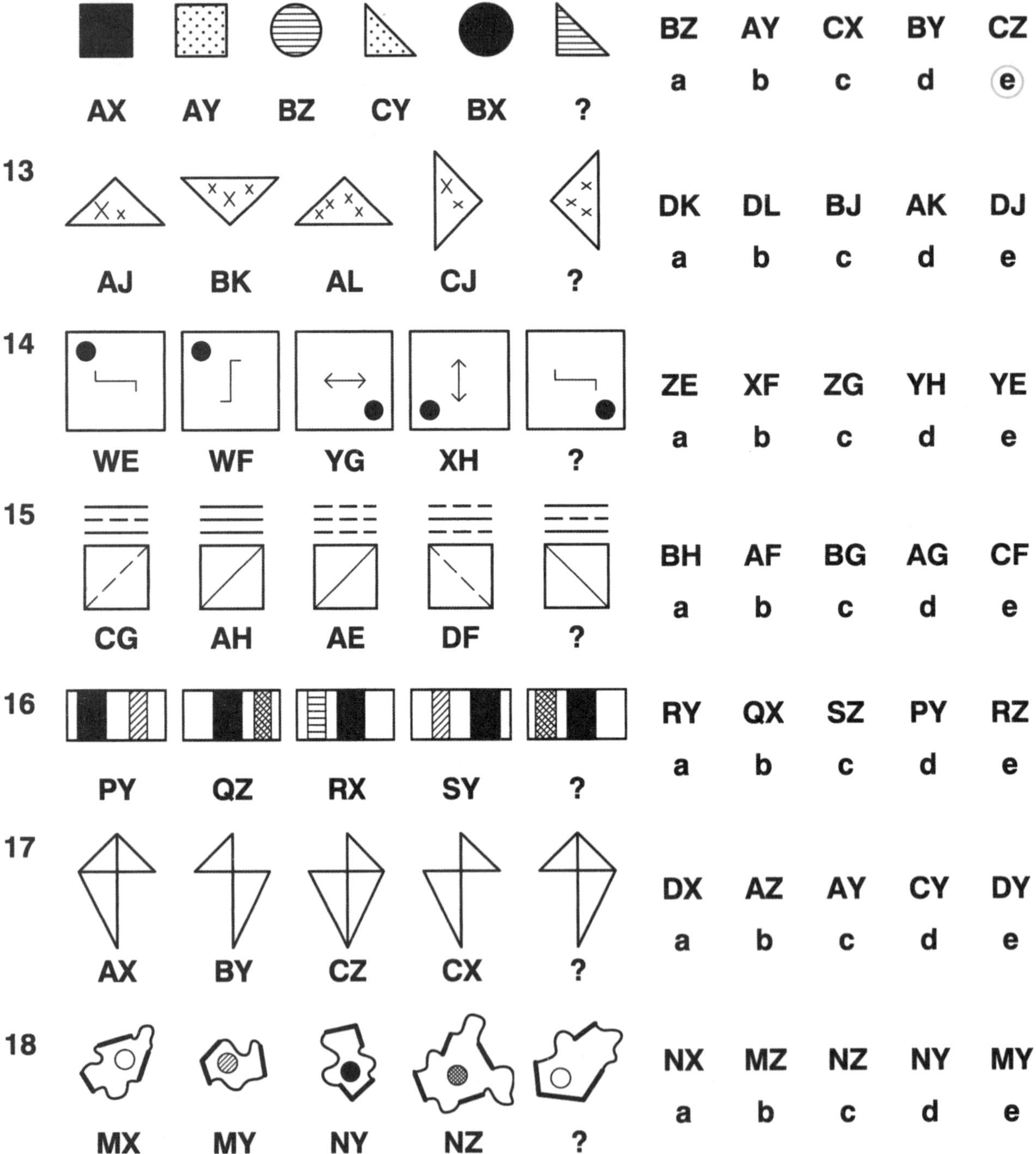

Which cube could not be made from the given net? Circle the letter.

Example

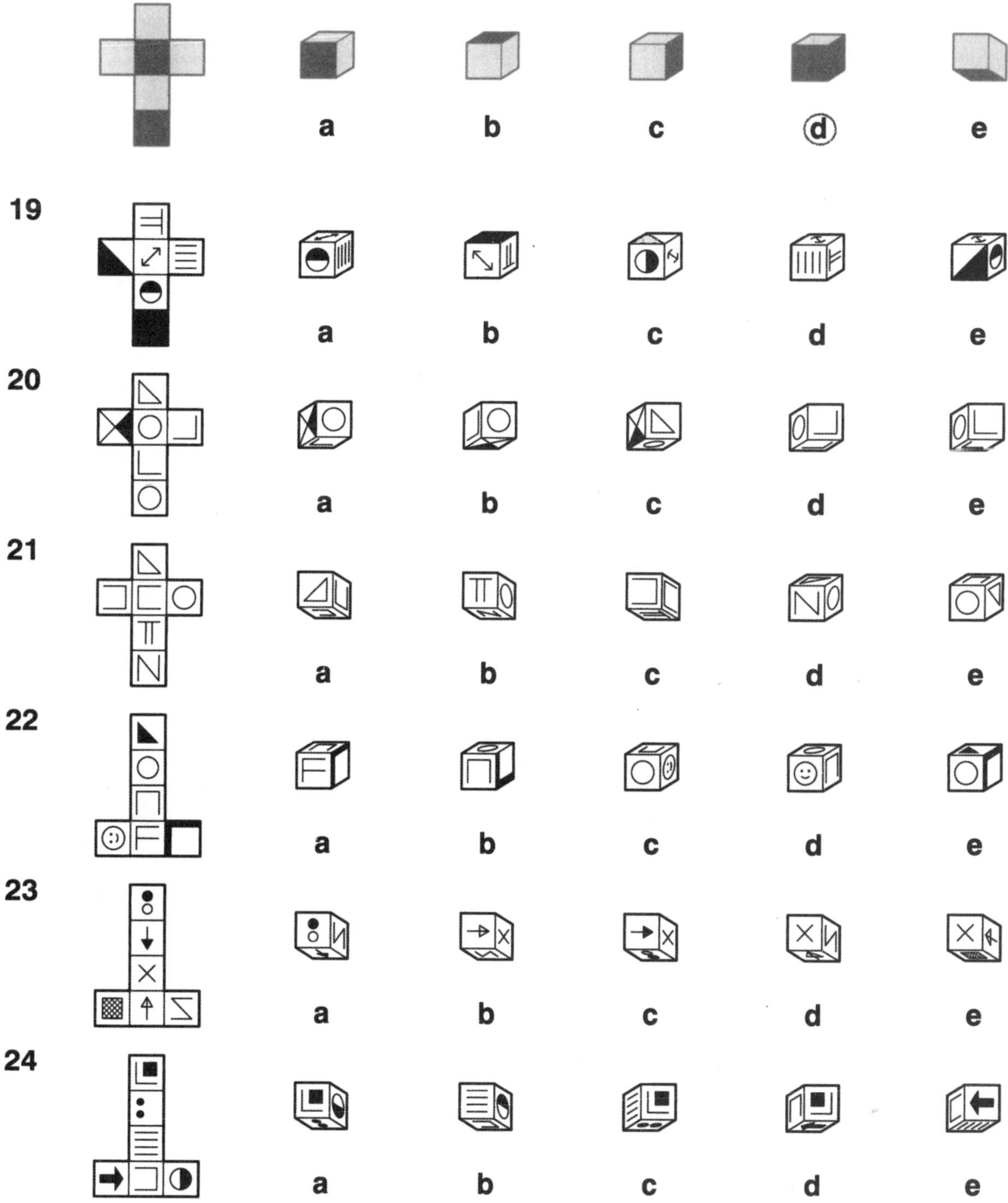

Which shape or pattern is a reflection of the shape on the left? Circle the letter.

Example

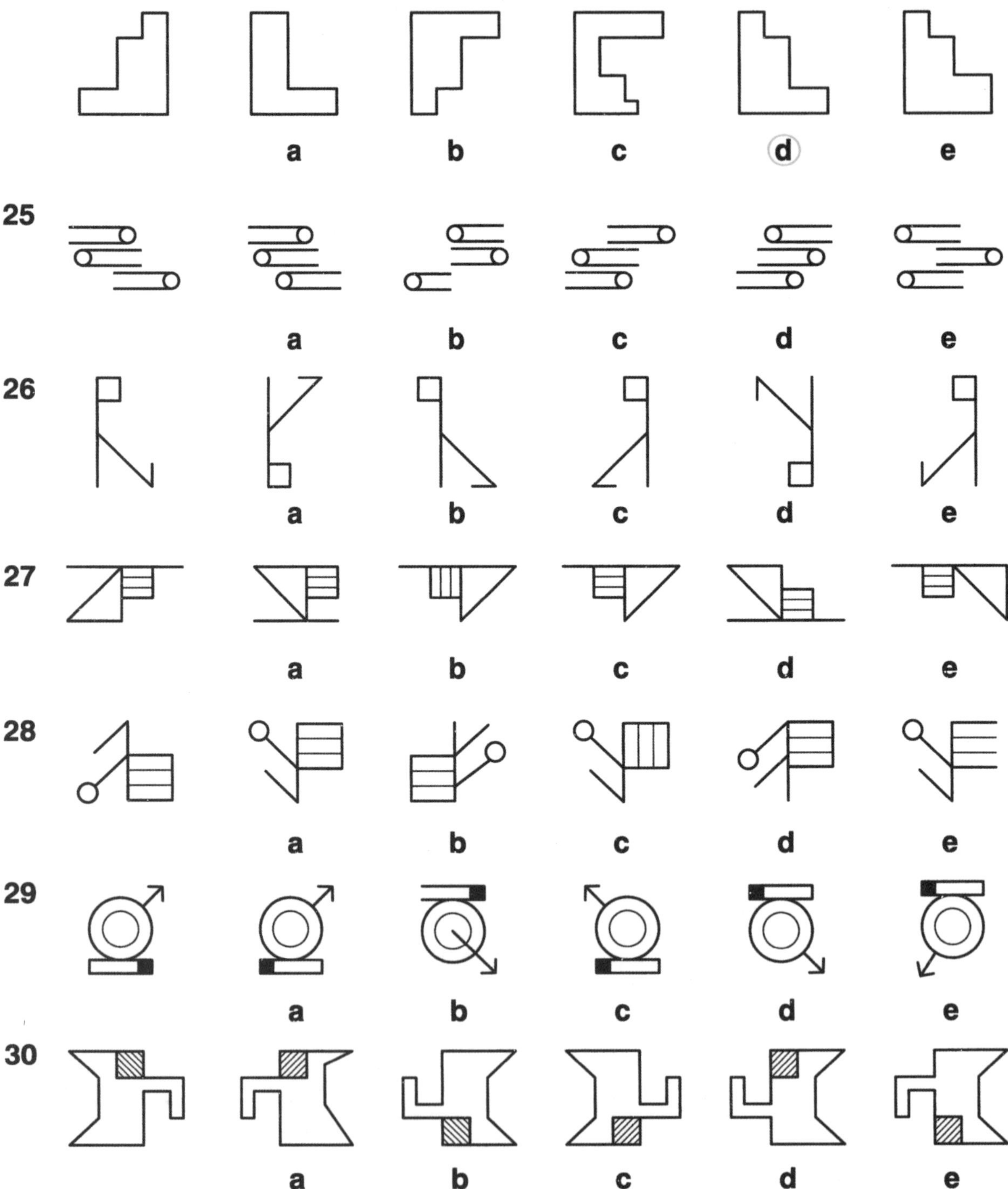

a   b   c   d   e

25

a   b   c   d   e

26

a   b   c   d   e

27

a   b   c   d   e

28

a   b   c   d   e

29

a   b   c   d   e

30

a   b   c   d   e

Which shape or pattern continues or completes the given sequence?
Circle the letter.

Example

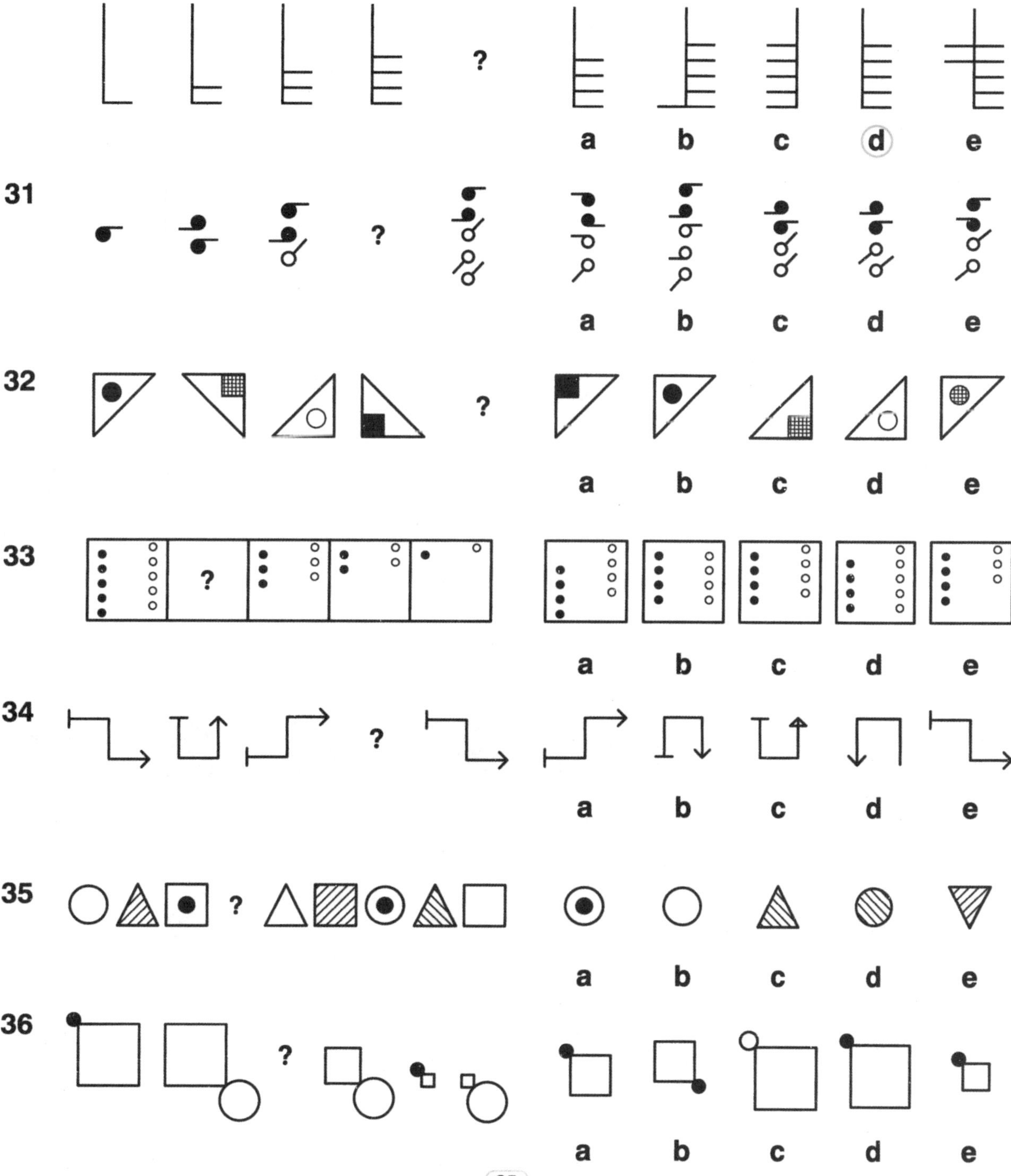

Which shape or pattern completes the grid on the left? Circle the letter.

Example

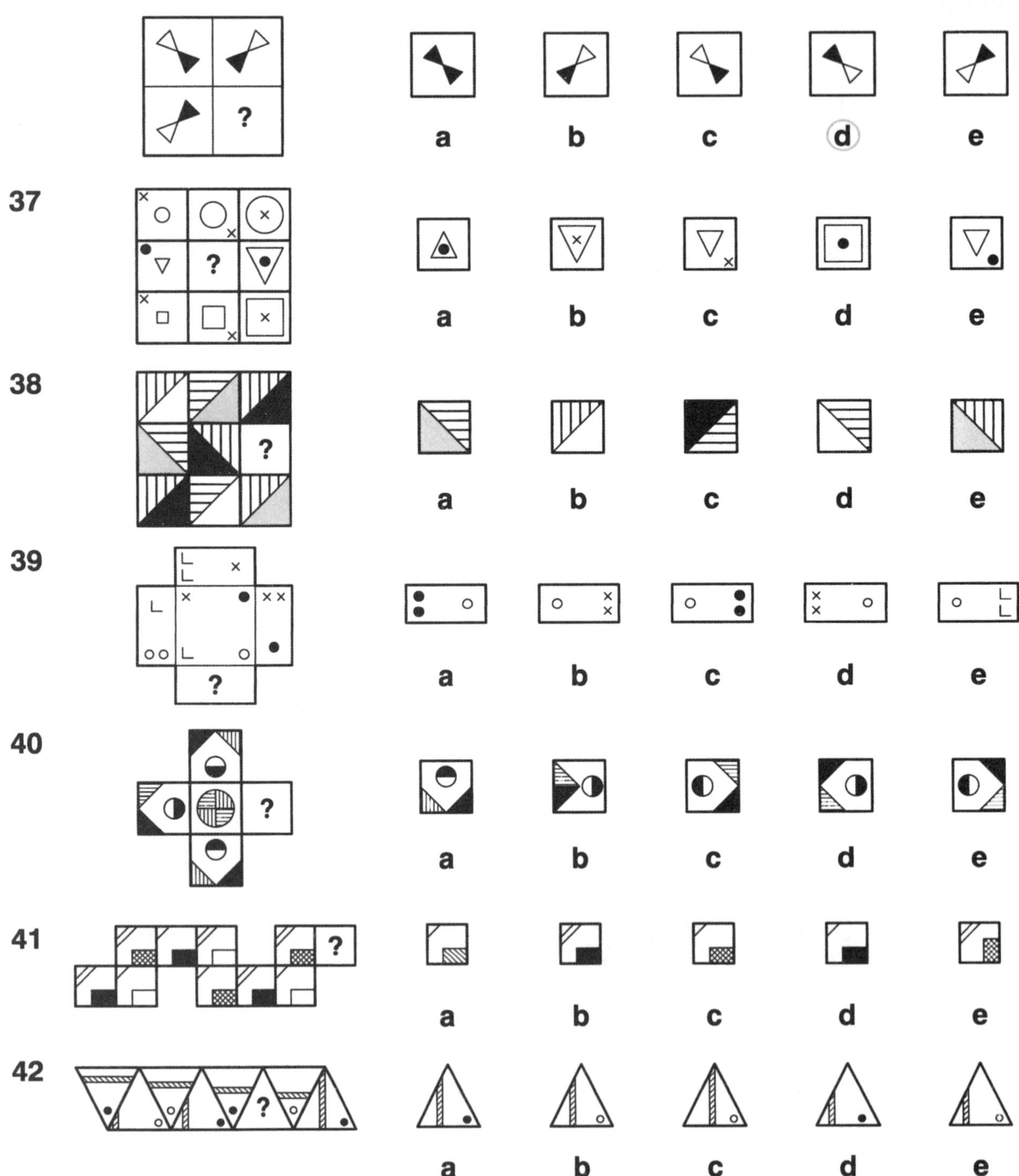

Focus test 1: Similarities

1 b
2 c
3 e
4 a
5 c
6 e
7 d
8 e
9 d
10 c
11 e
12 d

Focus test 2: Analogies

1 b
2 d
3 e
4 e
5 c
6 d
7 e
8 d
9 e
10 e
11 b
12 b

Focus test 3: Codes

1 d
2 c
3 e
4 c
5 e
6 c
7 a
8 c
9 e
10 c
11 c
12 e

Focus test 4: Cubes

1 b
2 c
3 e
4 c
5 e
6 e
7 d
8 d
9 b
10 c
11 c
12 d

Bond Non-verbal Reasoning Assessment Papers Stretch 9–10 years

Focus test 5: Reflections

1 d
2 e
3 c
4 e
5 b
6 e
7 c
8 c
9 e
10 c
11 d
12 b

Focus test 7: Grids

1 e
2 b
3 d
4 e
5 b
6 d
7 d
8 e
9 c
10 e
11 d
12 e

Focus test 6: Sequences

1 e
2 e
3 d
4 e
5 b
6 c
7 d
8 c
9 d
10 e
11 b
12 e

Focus test 8: Combining shapes

1 e
2 c
3 c
4 d
5 c
6 d
7 a
8 e
9 e
10 d
11 c
12 c

Mixed paper 1

1 d	**25** c
2 e	**26** e
3 e	**27** d
4 d	**28** a
5 c	**29** c
6 d	**30** c
7 e	**31** d
8 d	**32** e
9 b	**33** c
10 d	**34** b
11 e	**35** d
12 b	**36** a
13 a	**37** e
14 e	**38** d
15 c	**39** c
16 e	**40** e
17 c	**41** d
18 d	**42** b
19 b	**43** d
20 e	**44** d
21 d	**45** b
22 e	**46** e
23 c	**47** c
24 c	**48** e

Mixed paper 2

1 c	**25** b
2 d	**26** d
3 e	**27** e
4 a	**28** d
5 c	**29** c
6 b	**30** d
7 c	**31** a
8 c	**32** c
9 d	**33** b
10 c	**34** b
11 e	**35** d
12 b	**36** e
13 a	**37** e
14 d	**38** b
15 b	**39** e
16 a	**40** c
17 c	**41** d
18 e	**42** a
19 c	**43** d
20 c	**44** e
21 b	**45** d
22 e	**46** e
23 c	**47** b
24 d	**48** c

Mixed paper 3

1 d	**25** c
2 e	**26** c
3 d	**27** b
4 e	**28** d
5 a	**29** c
6 c	**30** d
7 b	**31** c
8 e	**32** a
9 e	**33** b
10 d	**34** d
11 c	**35** b
12 a	**36** e
13 c	**37** d
14 b	**38** e
15 d	**39** d
16 b	**40** c
17 d	**41** b
18 a	**42** c
19 c	**43** a
20 d	**44** d
21 c	**45** e
22 e	**46** b
23 e	**47** b
24 d	**48** c

Mixed paper 4

1 d	**25** c
2 e	**26** c
3 c	**27** b
4 c	**28** c
5 a	**29** e
6 c	**30** d
7 e	**31** d
8 c	**32** a
9 d	**33** b
10 d	**34** e
11 b	**35** b
12 c	**36** e
13 b	**37** e
14 c	**38** c
15 d	**39** c
16 e	**40** d
17 c	**41** a
18 d	**42** e
19 d	**43** d
20 b	**44** d
21 e	**45** a
22 e	**46** b
23 b	**47** e
24 c	**48** a

Which pattern on the right is formed by combining the two shapes on the left?
Circle the letter.

Example

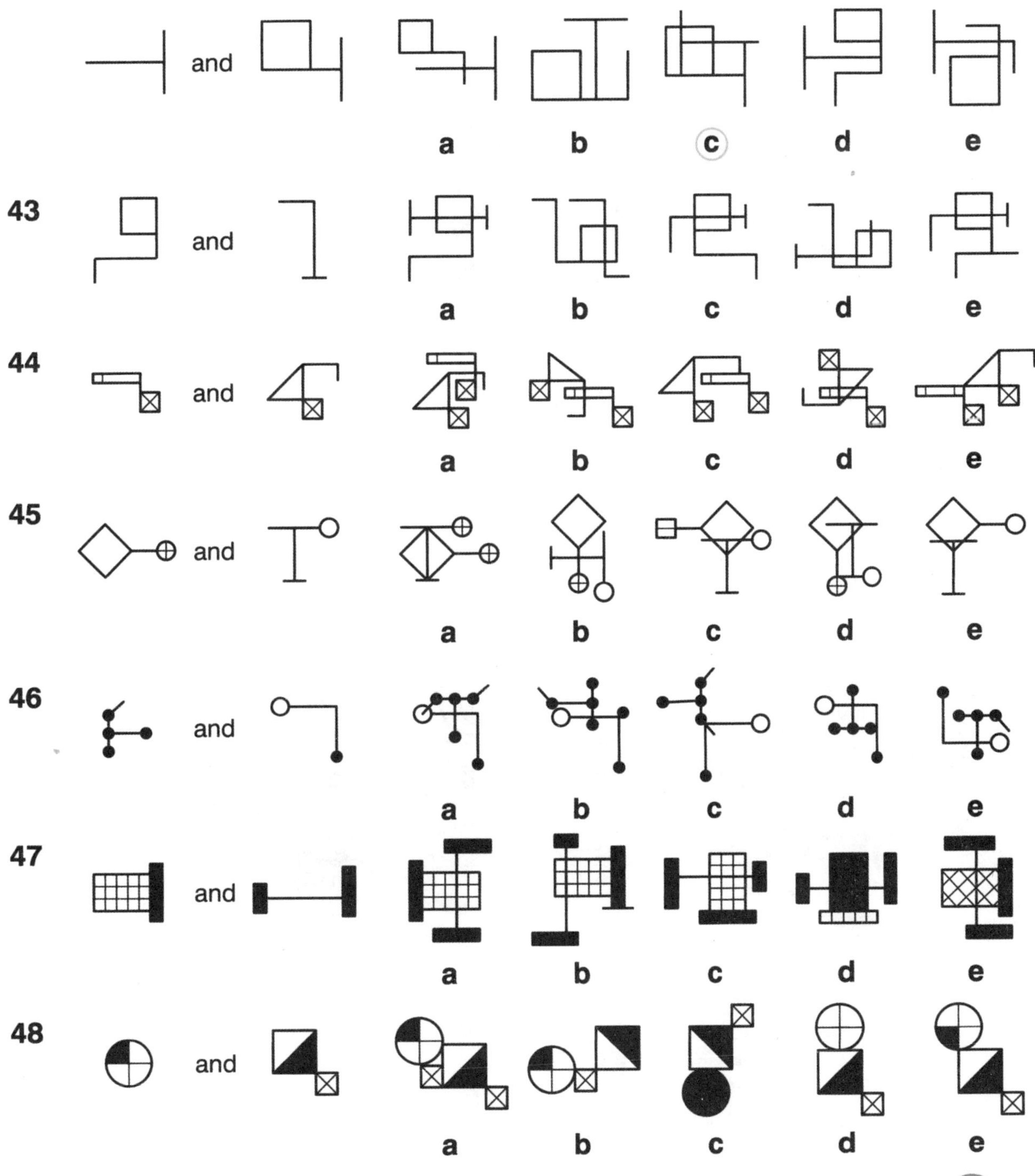

Mixed paper 2

Which of the shapes belongs to the group on the left? Circle the letter.

Example

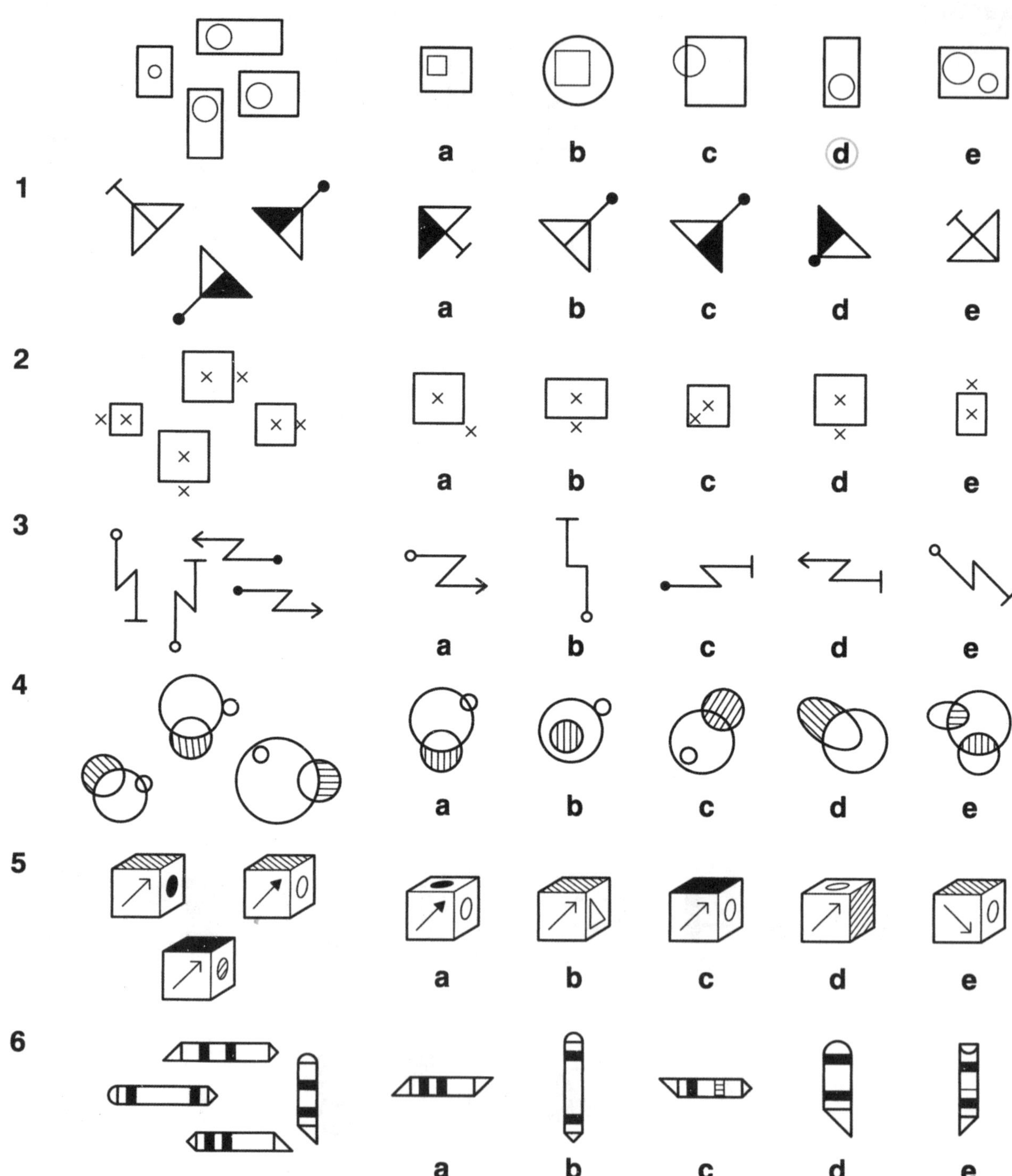

Which shape or pattern completes the second pair in the same way as the first pair? Circle the letter.

Example

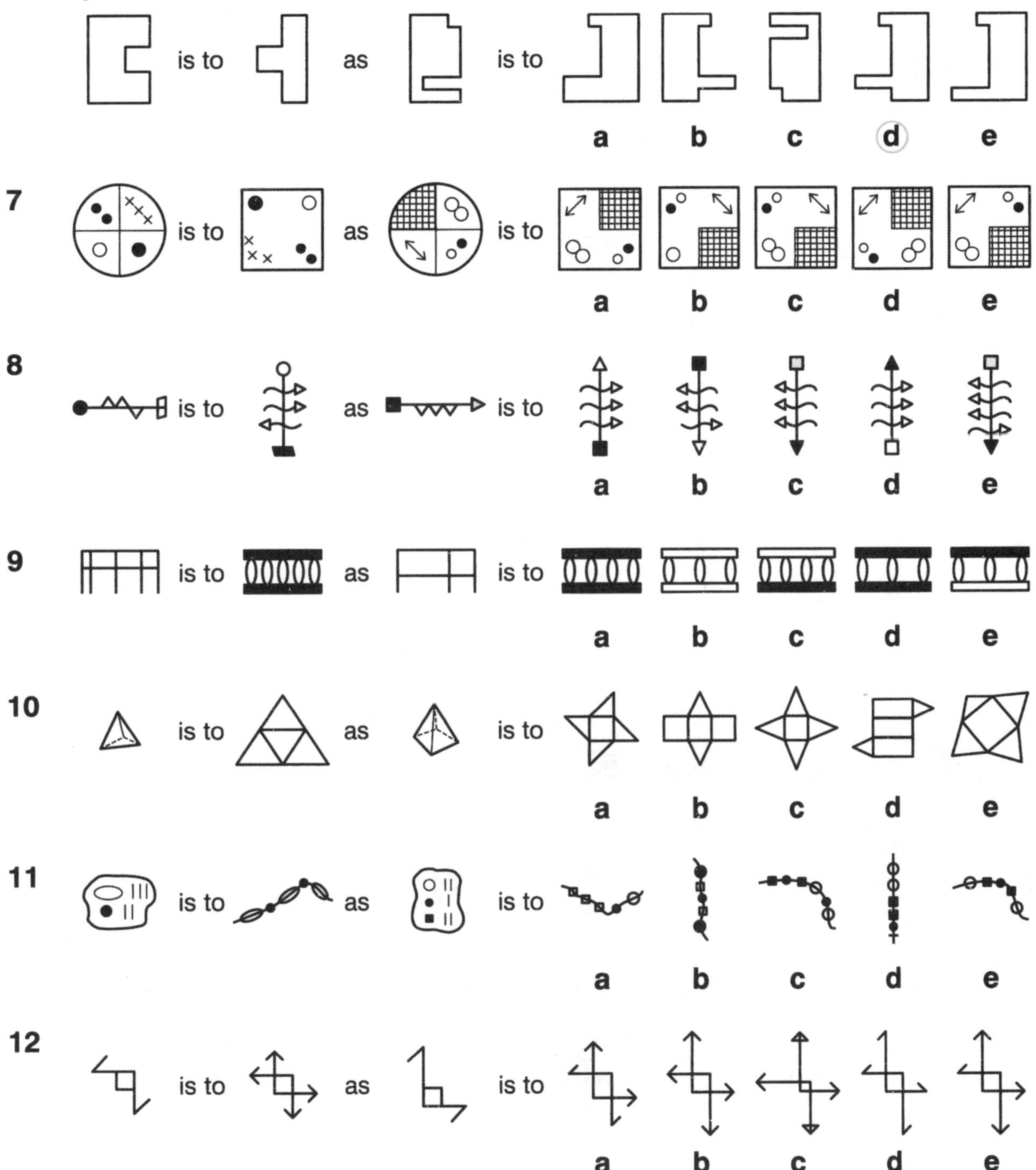

29

Using the given patterns and codes, work out the code that matches the last pattern. Circle the letter.

Example

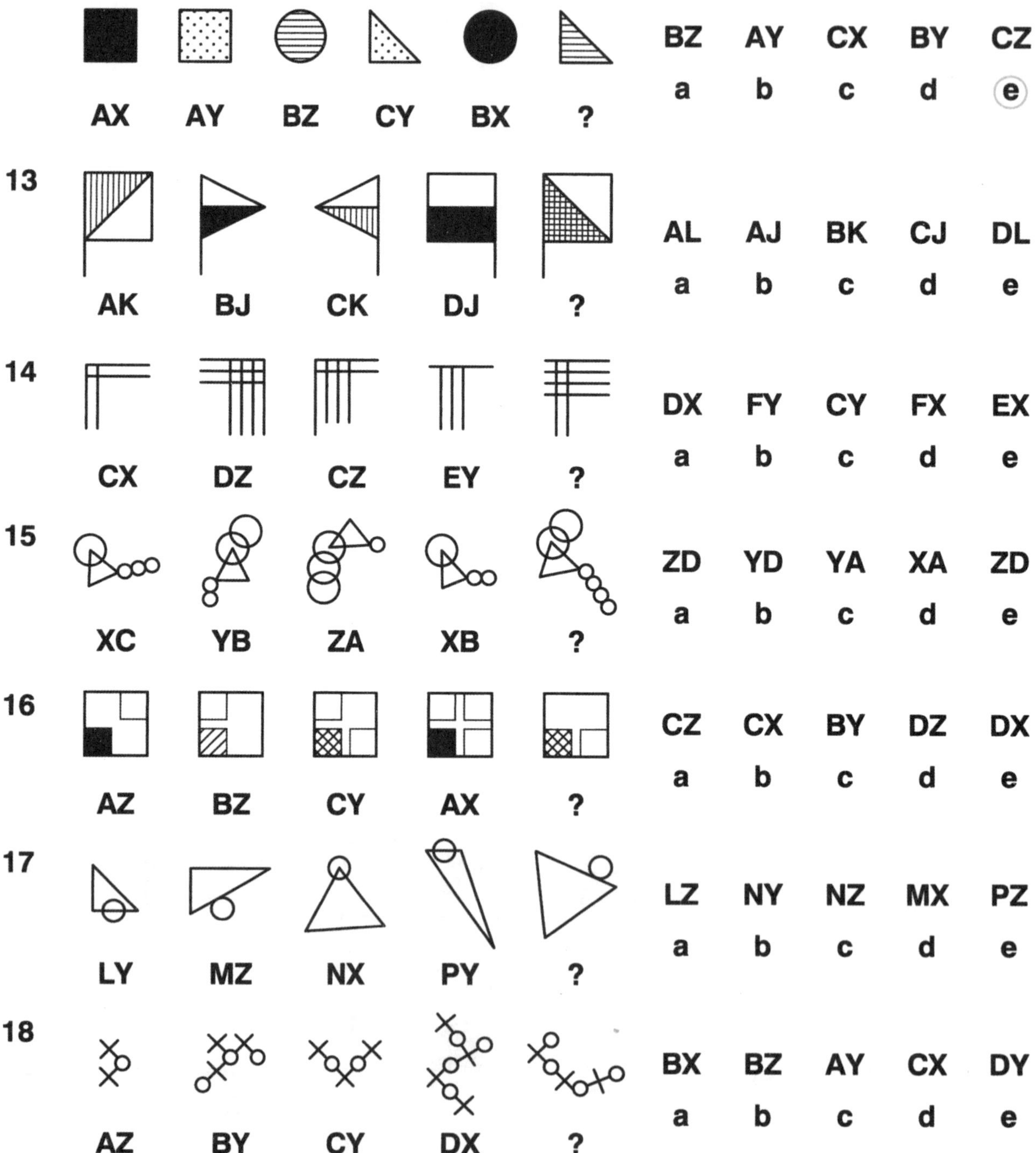

Which cube could not be made from the given net? Circle the letter.

Example

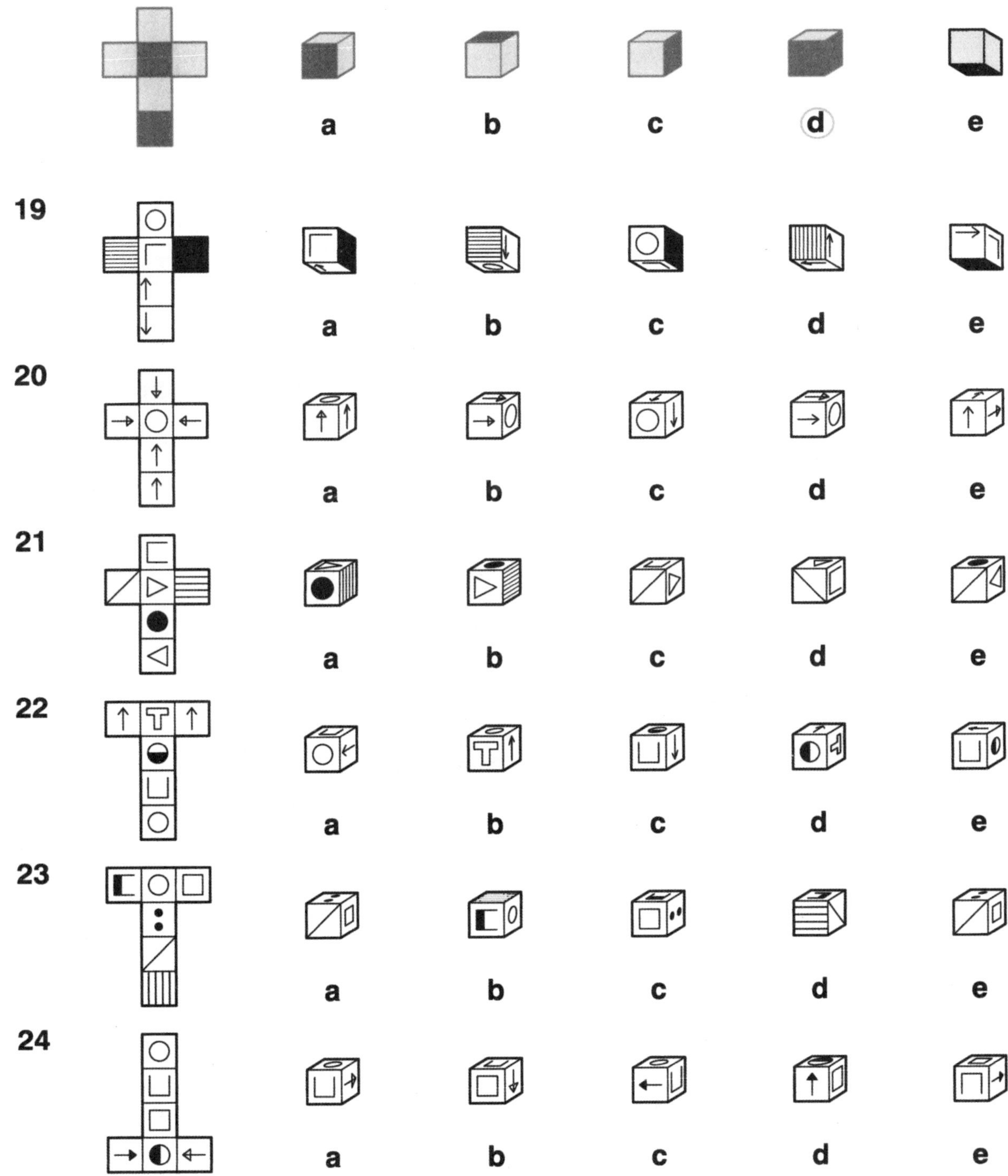

Which shape or pattern is a reflection of the shape on the left? Circle the letter.

Example

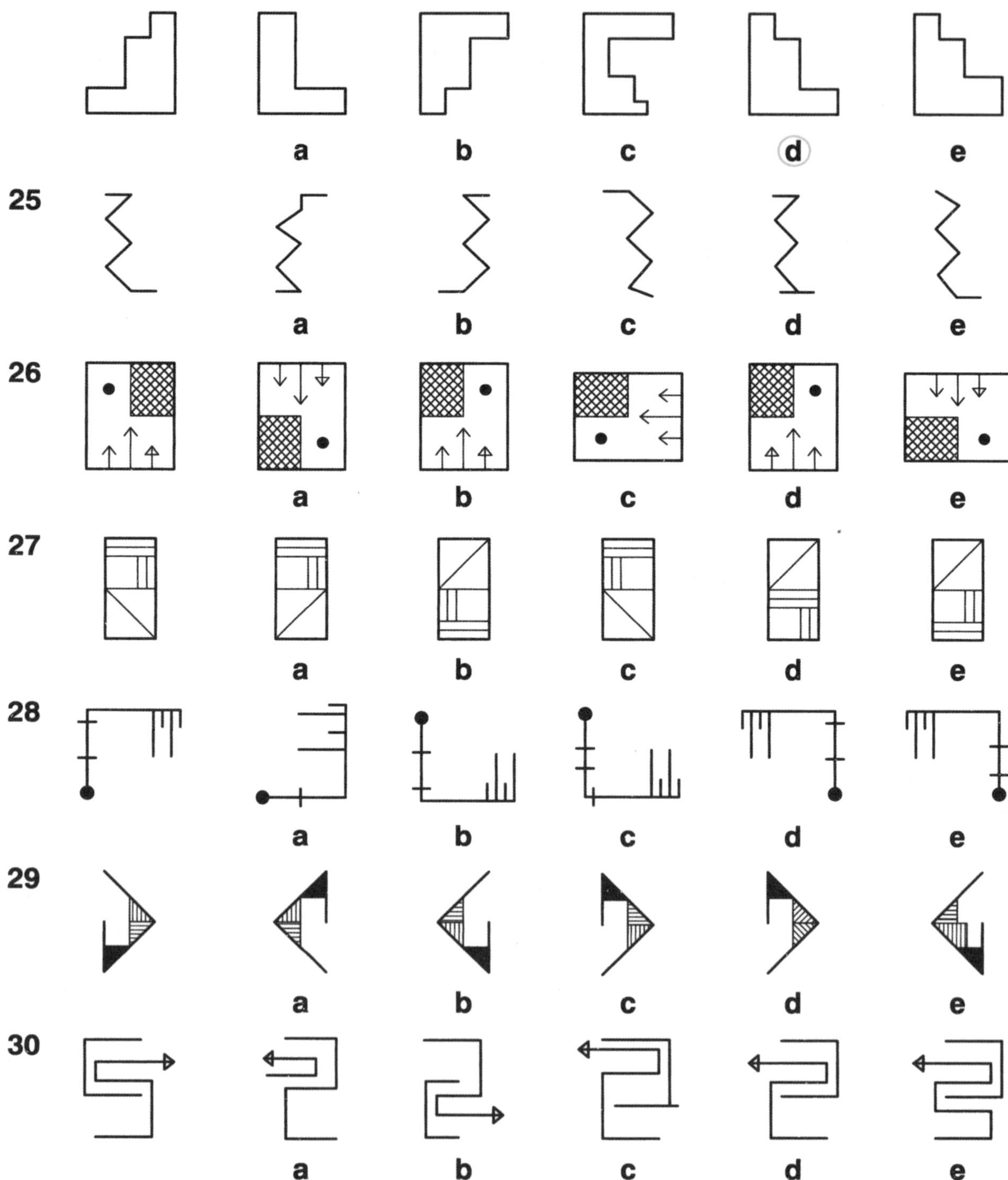

a b c (d) e

Which shape or pattern continues or completes the given sequence?
Circle the letter.

Example

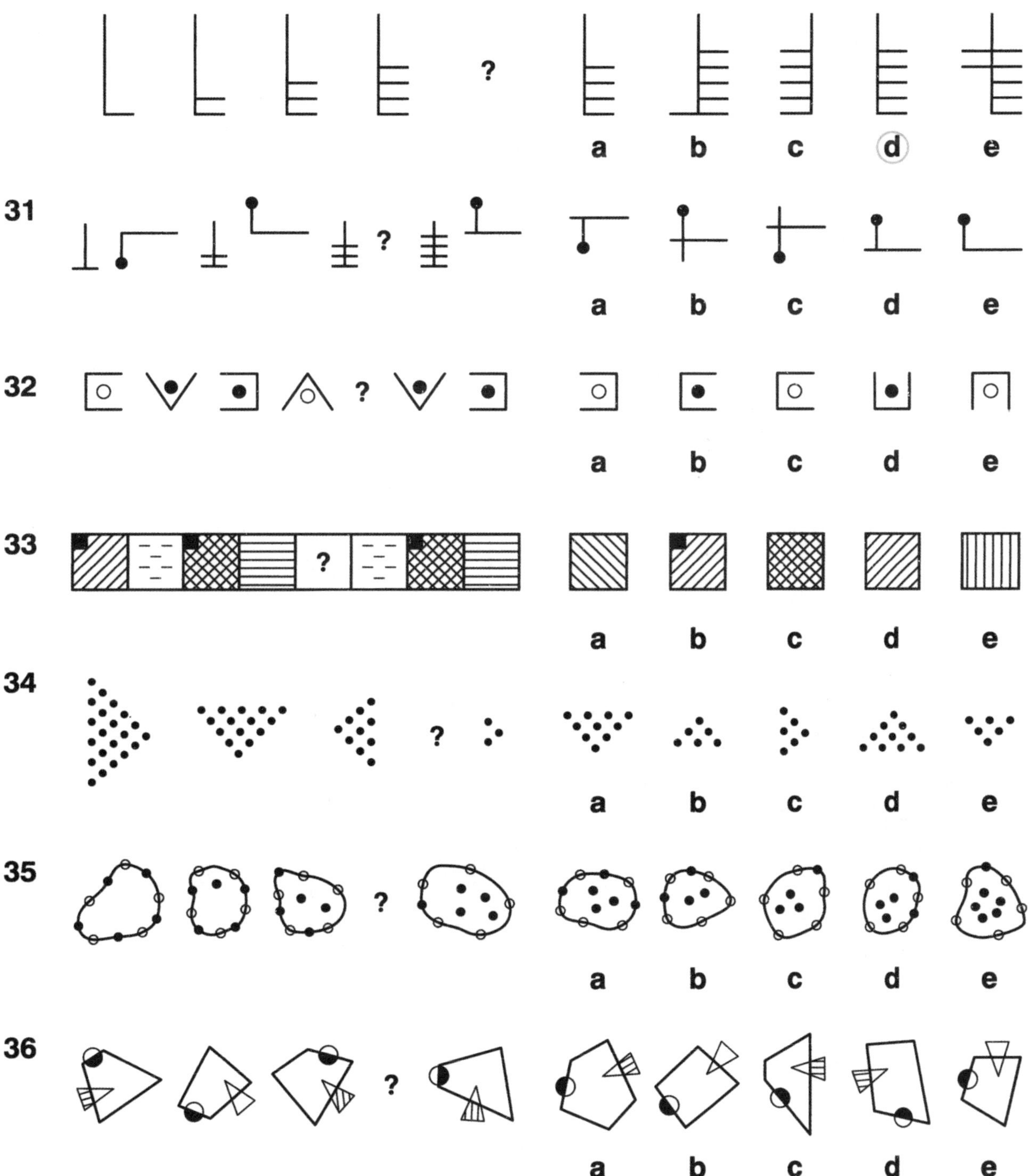

Which shape or pattern completes the grid on the left? Circle the letter.

Example

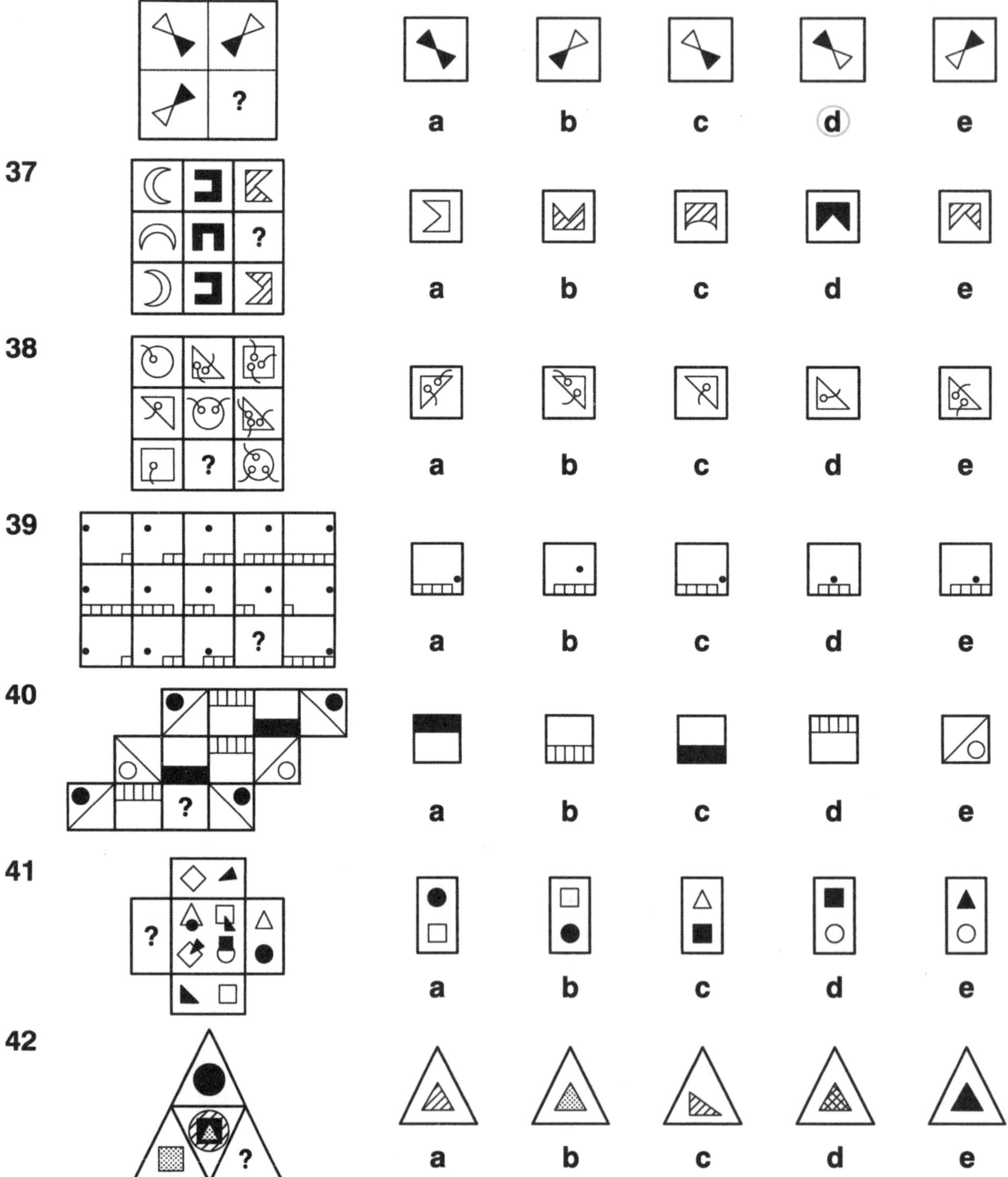

37

38

39

40

41

42

Which pattern on the right is formed by combining the two shapes on the left?
Circle the letter.

Example

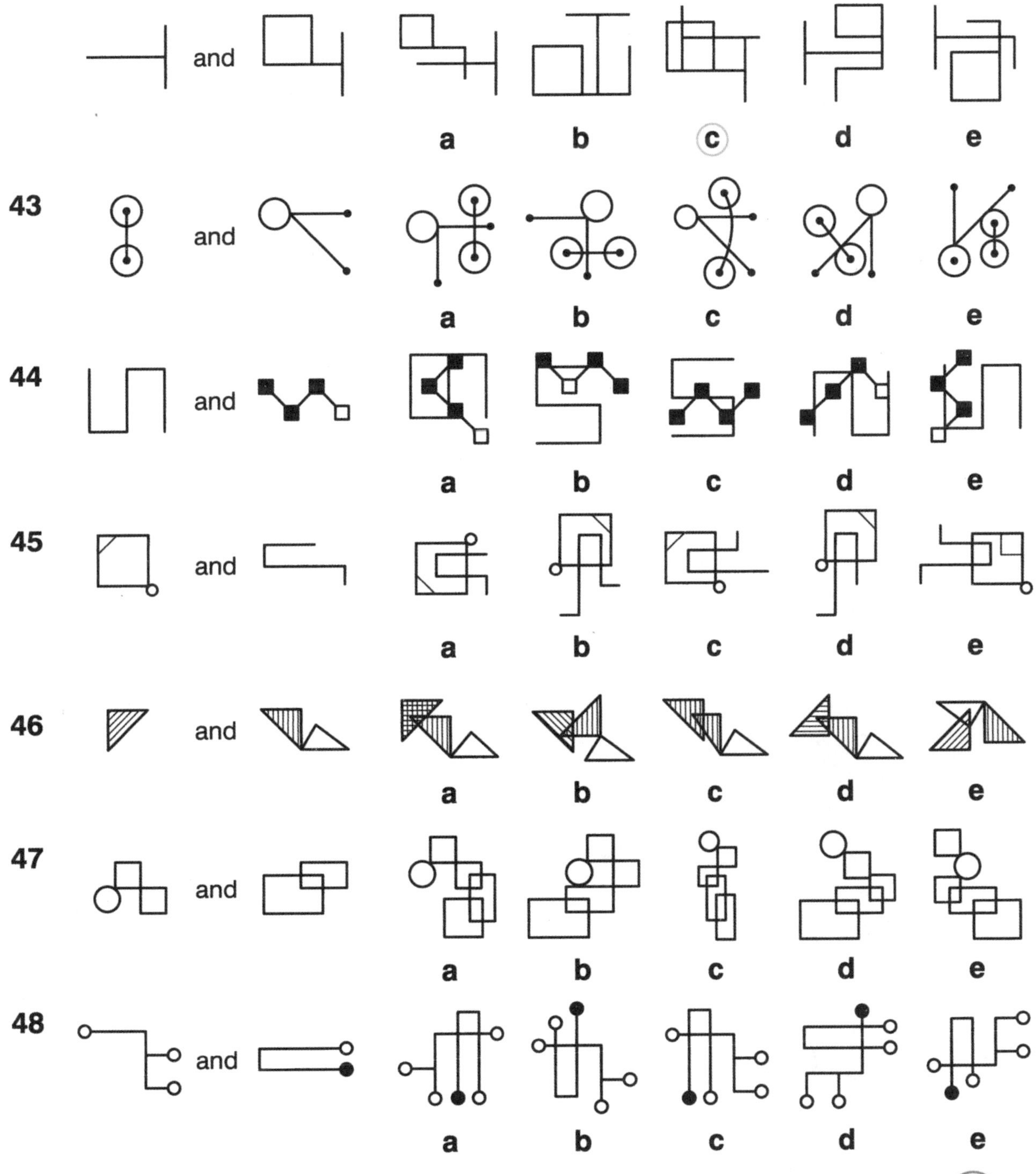

43

44

45

46

47

48

Mixed paper 3

Which of the shapes belongs to the group on the left? Circle the letter.

Example

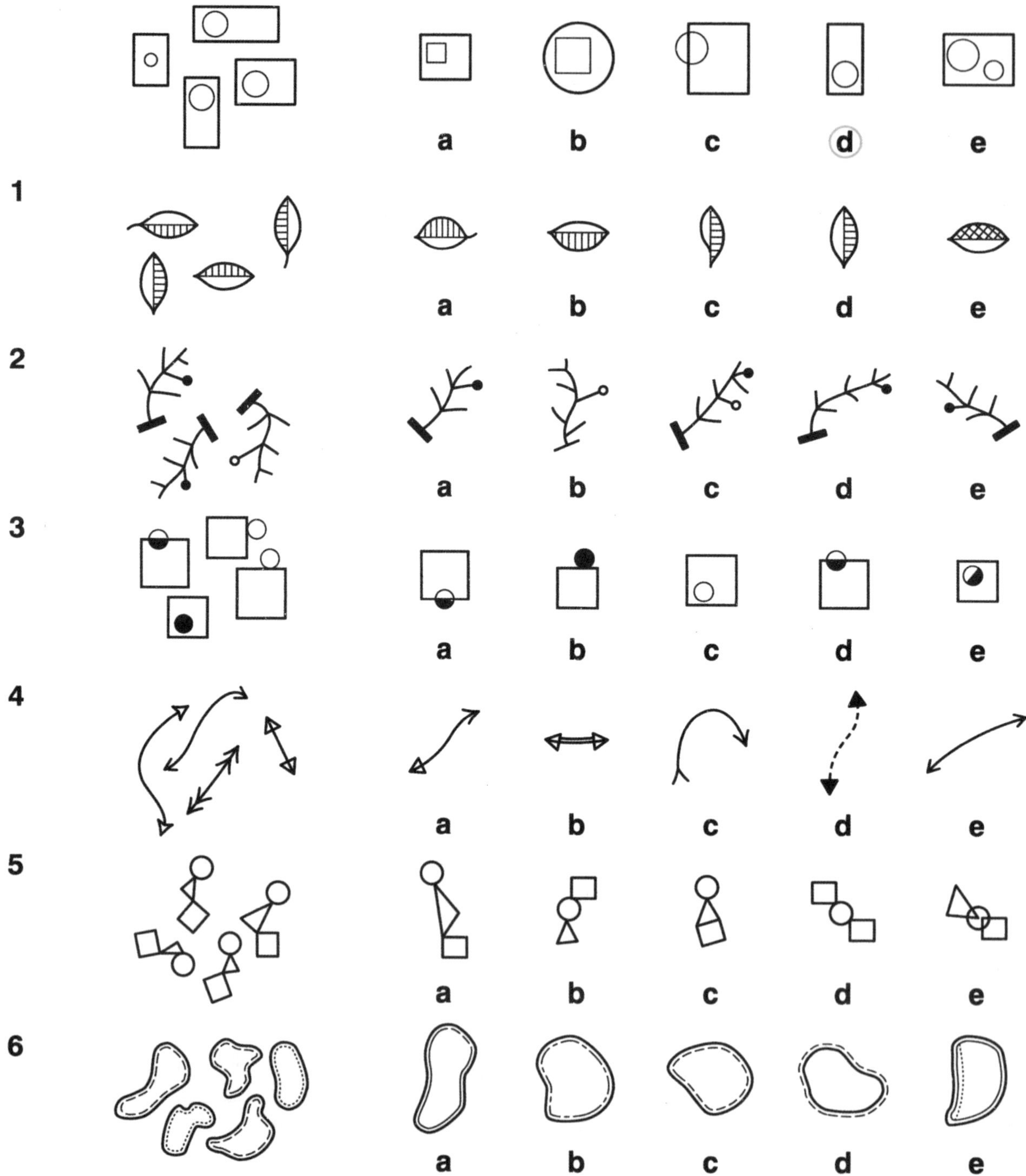

Which shape or pattern completes the second pair in the same way as the first pair? Circle the letter.

Example

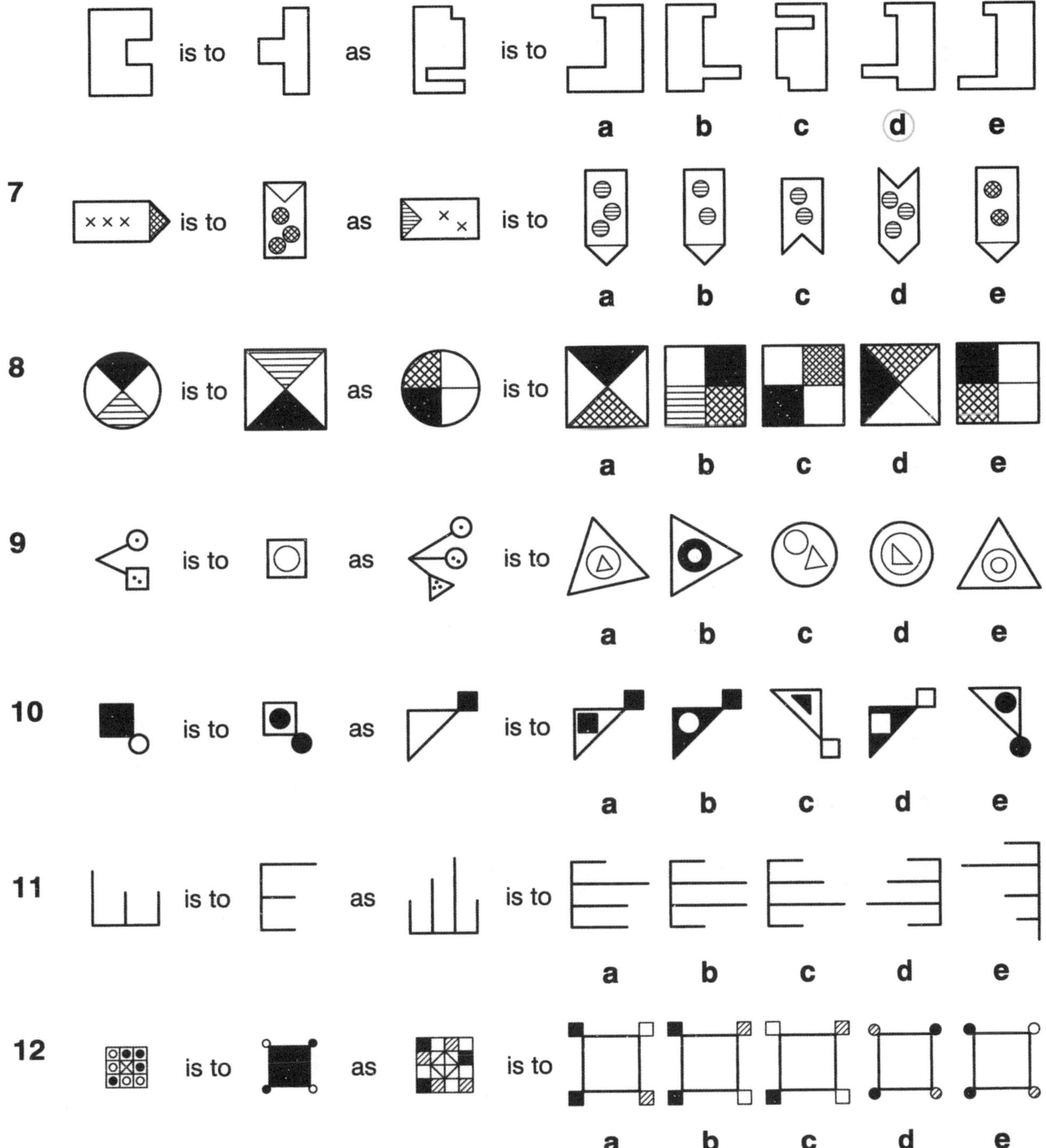

Using the given patterns and codes, work out the code that matches the last pattern. Circle the letter.

Example

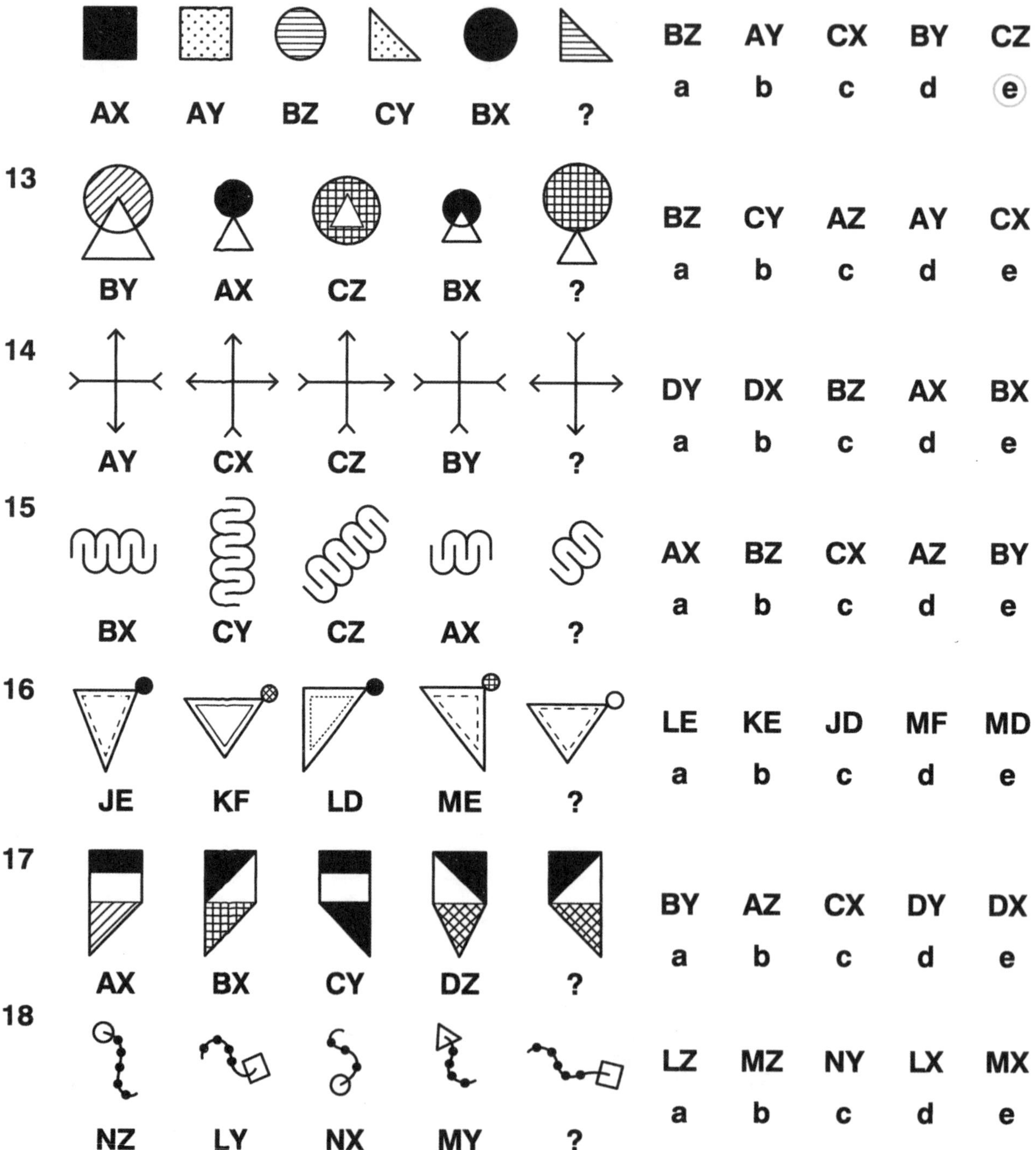

	BZ	AY	CX	BY	CZ
	a	b	c	d	(e)

13

	BZ	CY	AZ	AY	CX
	a	b	c	d	e

14

	DY	DX	BZ	AX	BX
	a	b	c	d	e

15

	AX	BZ	CX	AZ	BY
	a	b	c	d	e

16

	LE	KE	JD	MF	MD
	a	b	c	d	e

17

	BY	AZ	CX	DY	DX
	a	b	c	d	e

18

	LZ	MZ	NY	LX	MX
	a	b	c	d	e

Which cube could not be made from the given net? Circle the letter.

Example

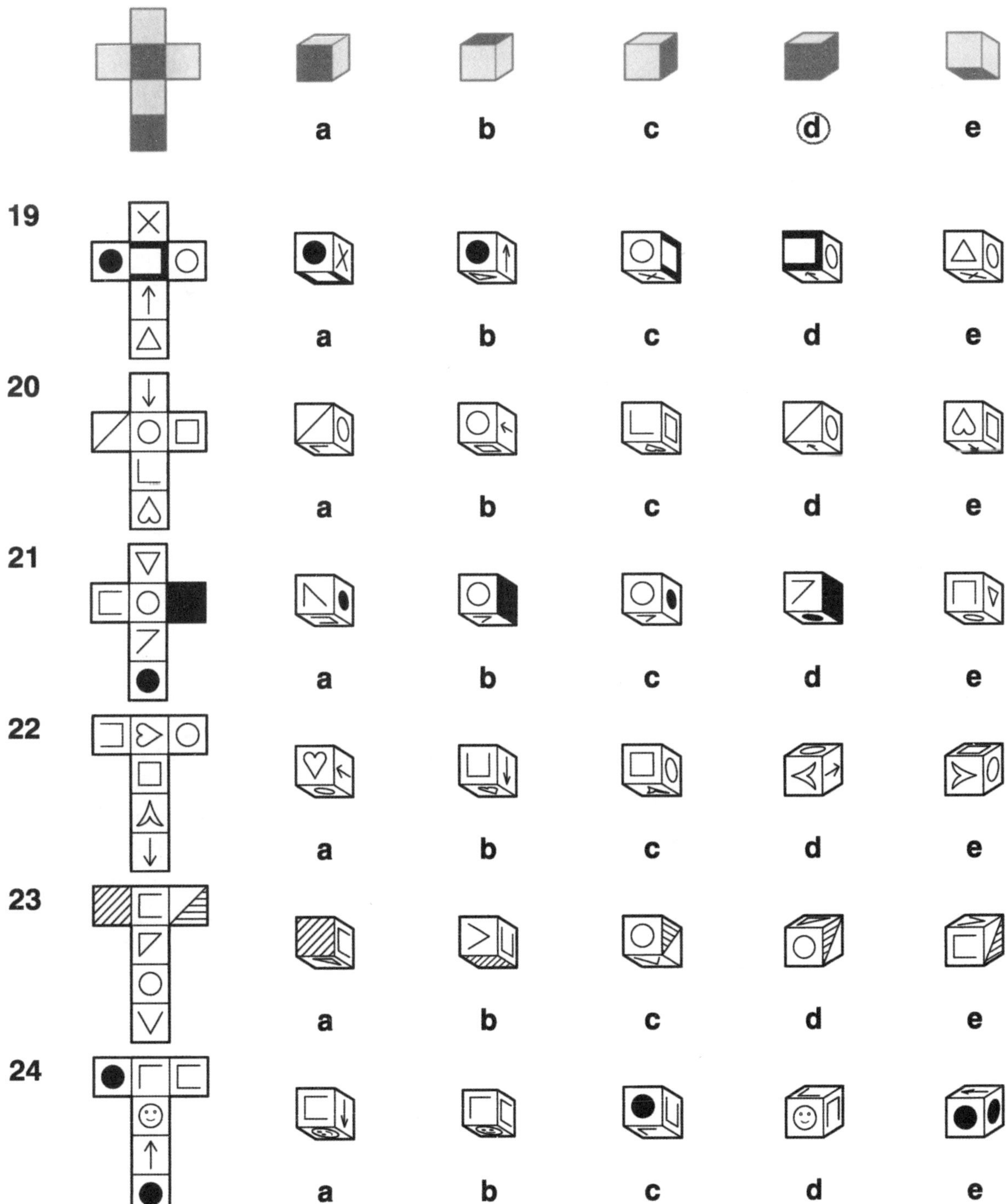

Which shape or pattern is a reflection of the shape on the left? Circle the letter.

Example

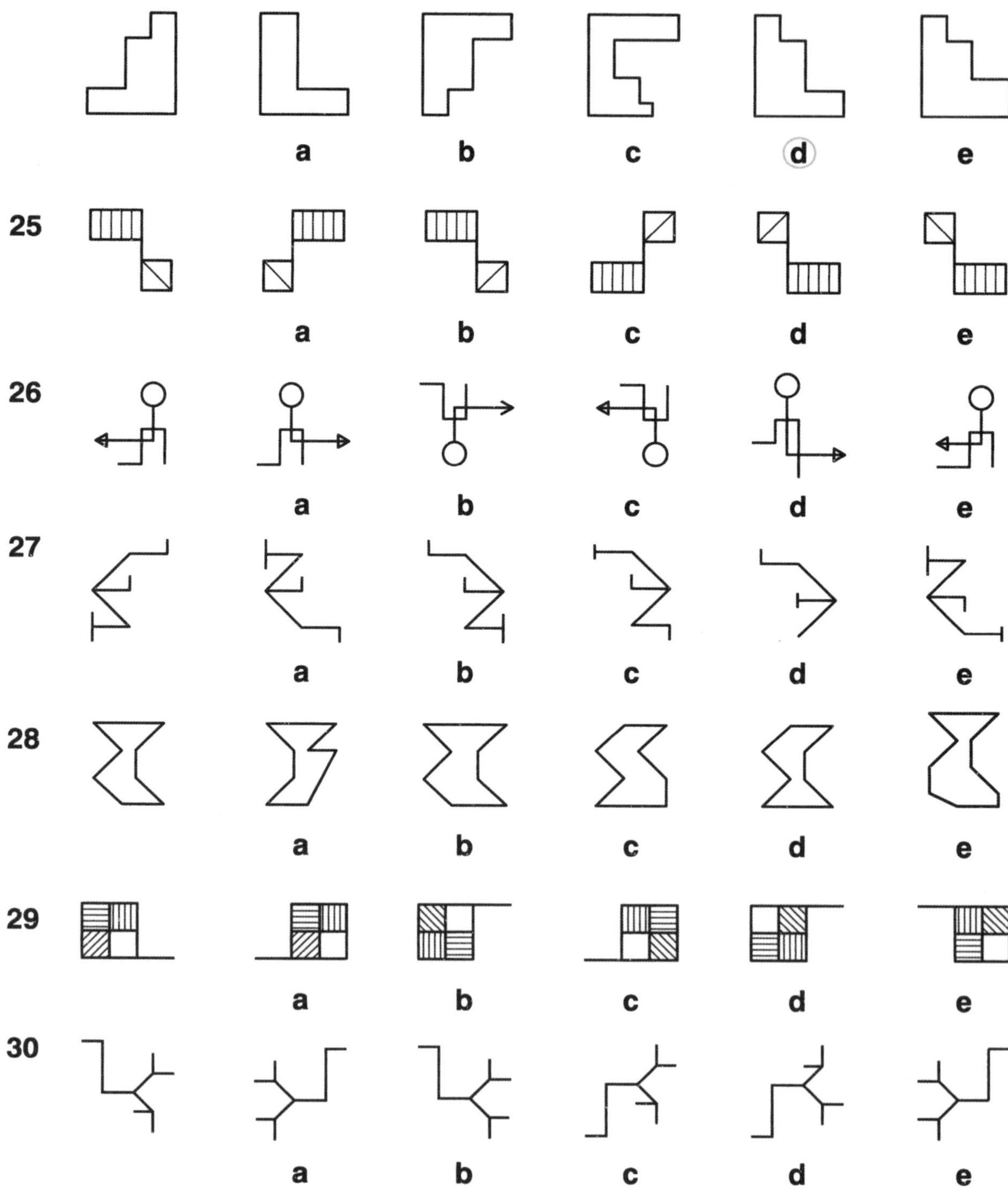

25

26

27

28

29

30

Which shape or pattern continues or completes the given sequence?
Circle the letter.

Example

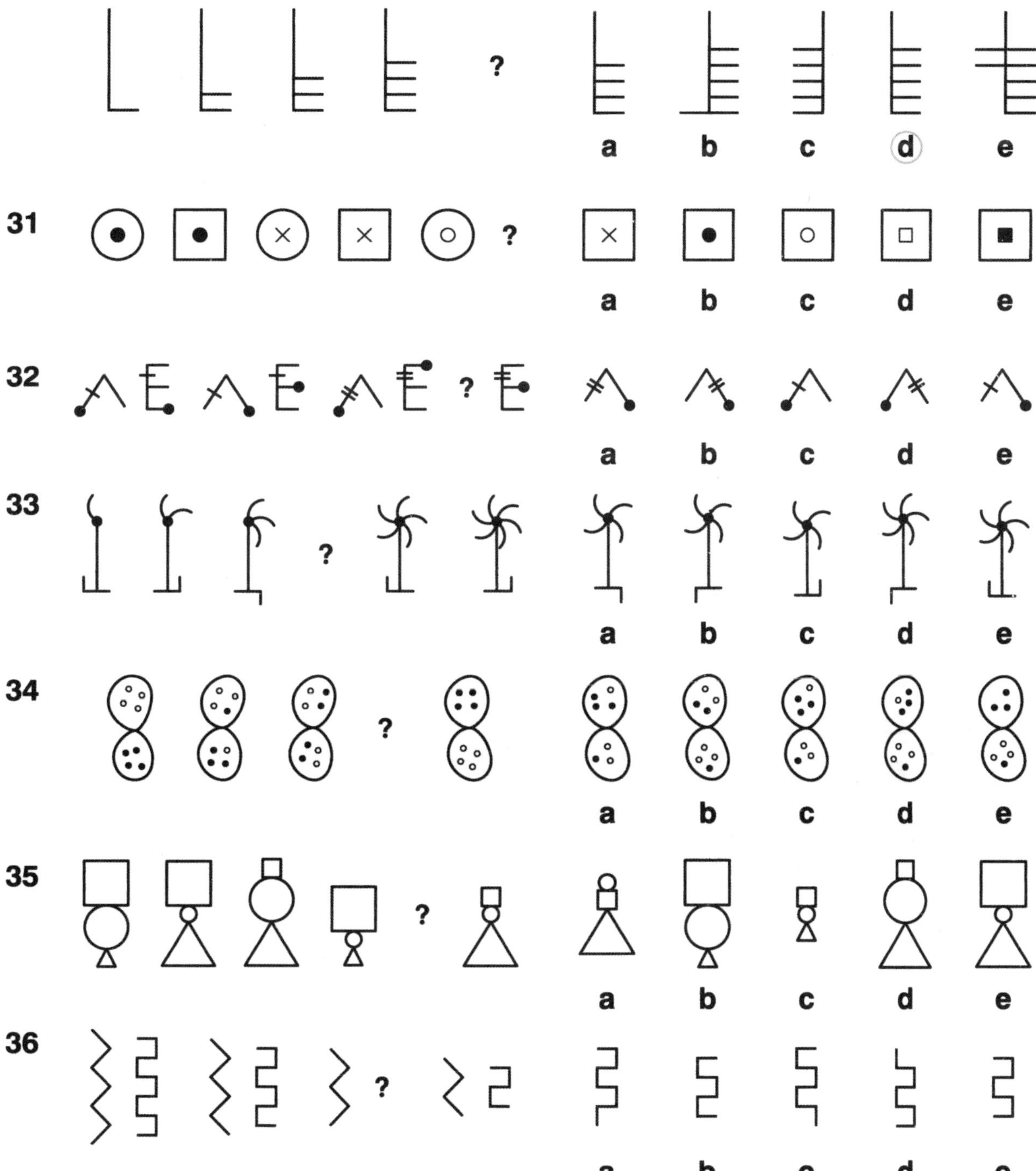

31

32

33

34

35

36

Which shape or pattern completes the grid on the left? Circle the letter.

Example

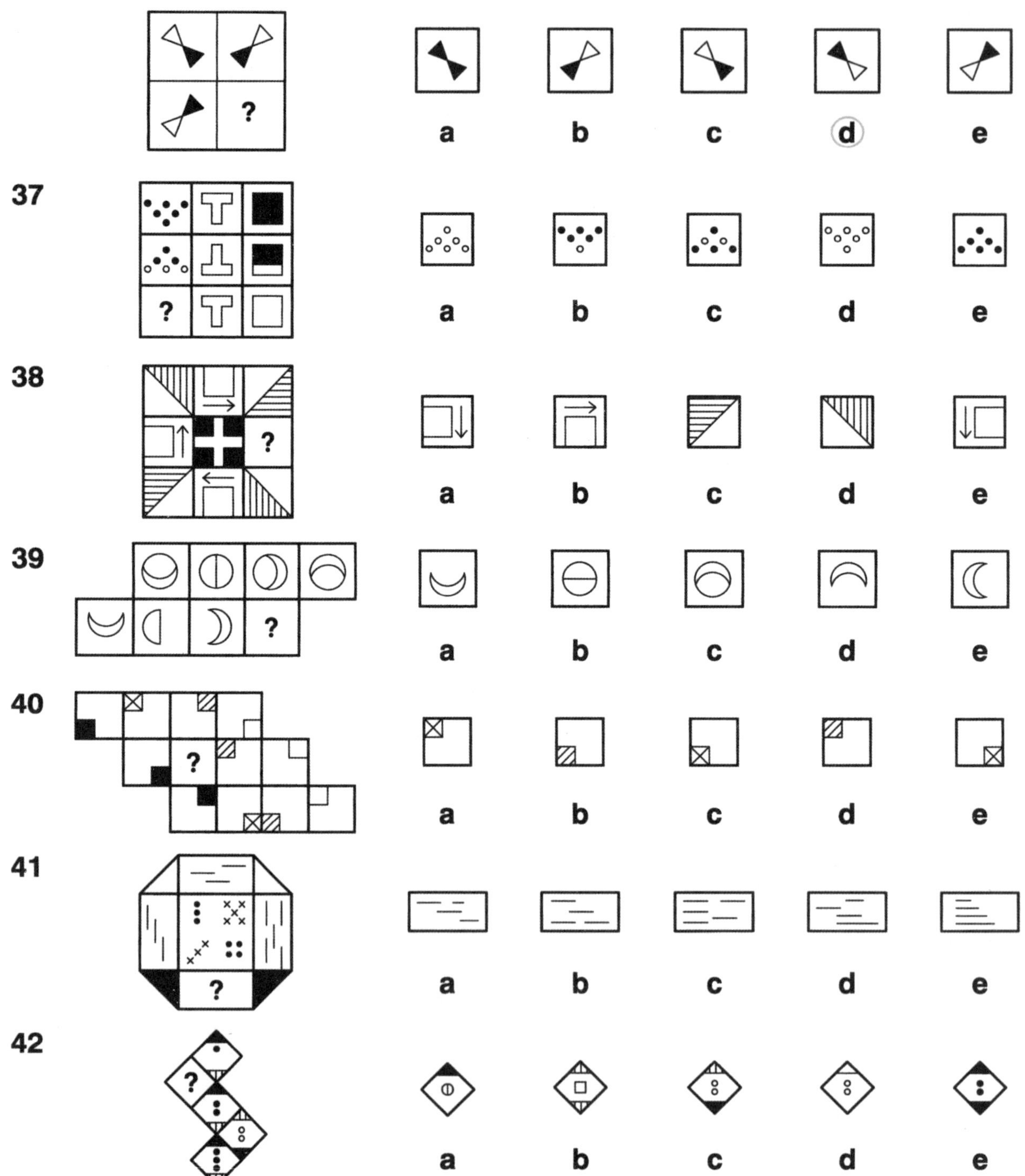

37

38

39

40

41

42

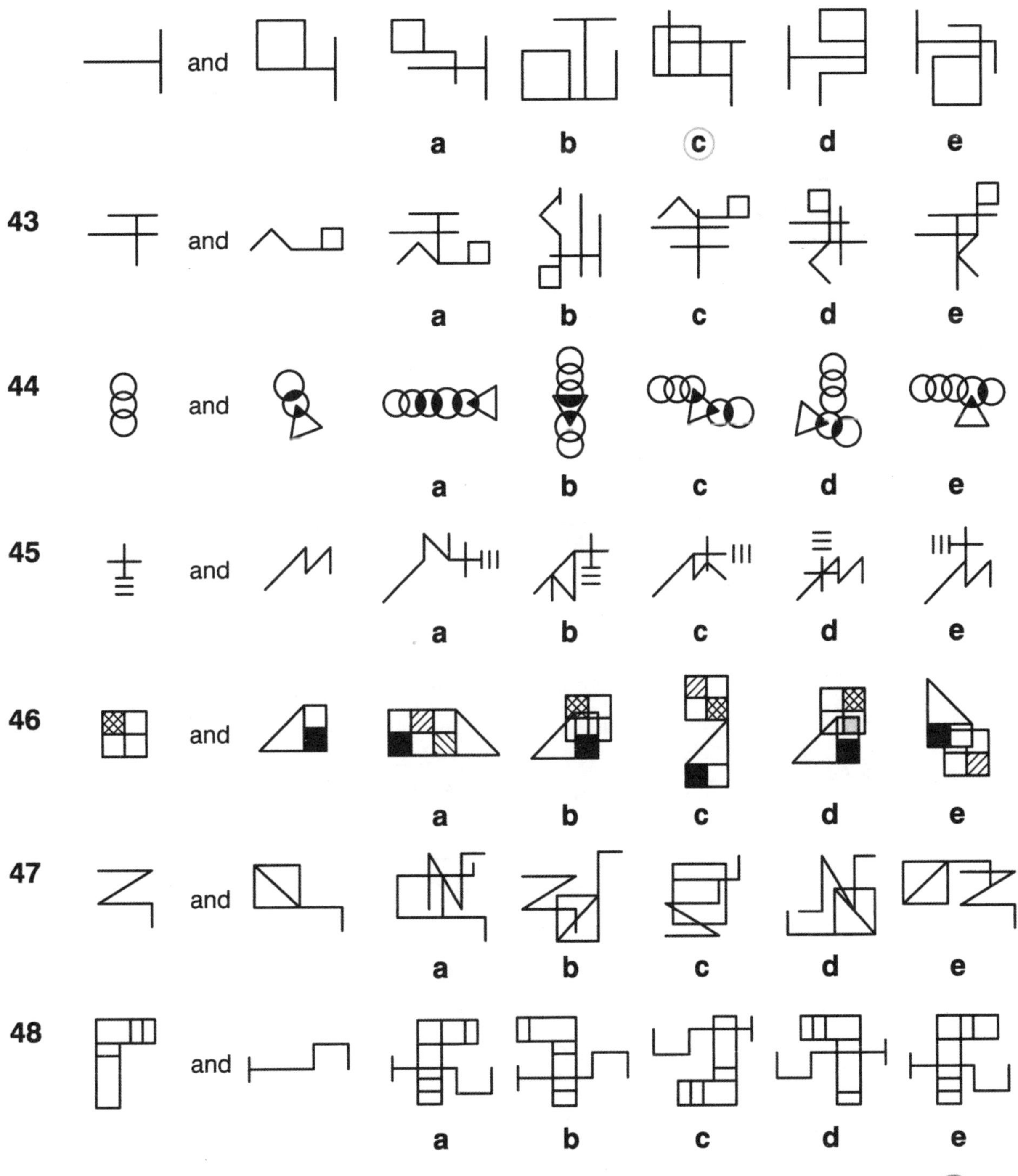

Which pattern on the right is formed by combining the two shapes on the left? Circle the letter.

Example

43

44

45

46

47

48

Mixed paper 4

Which of the shapes belongs to the group on the left? Circle the letter.

Example

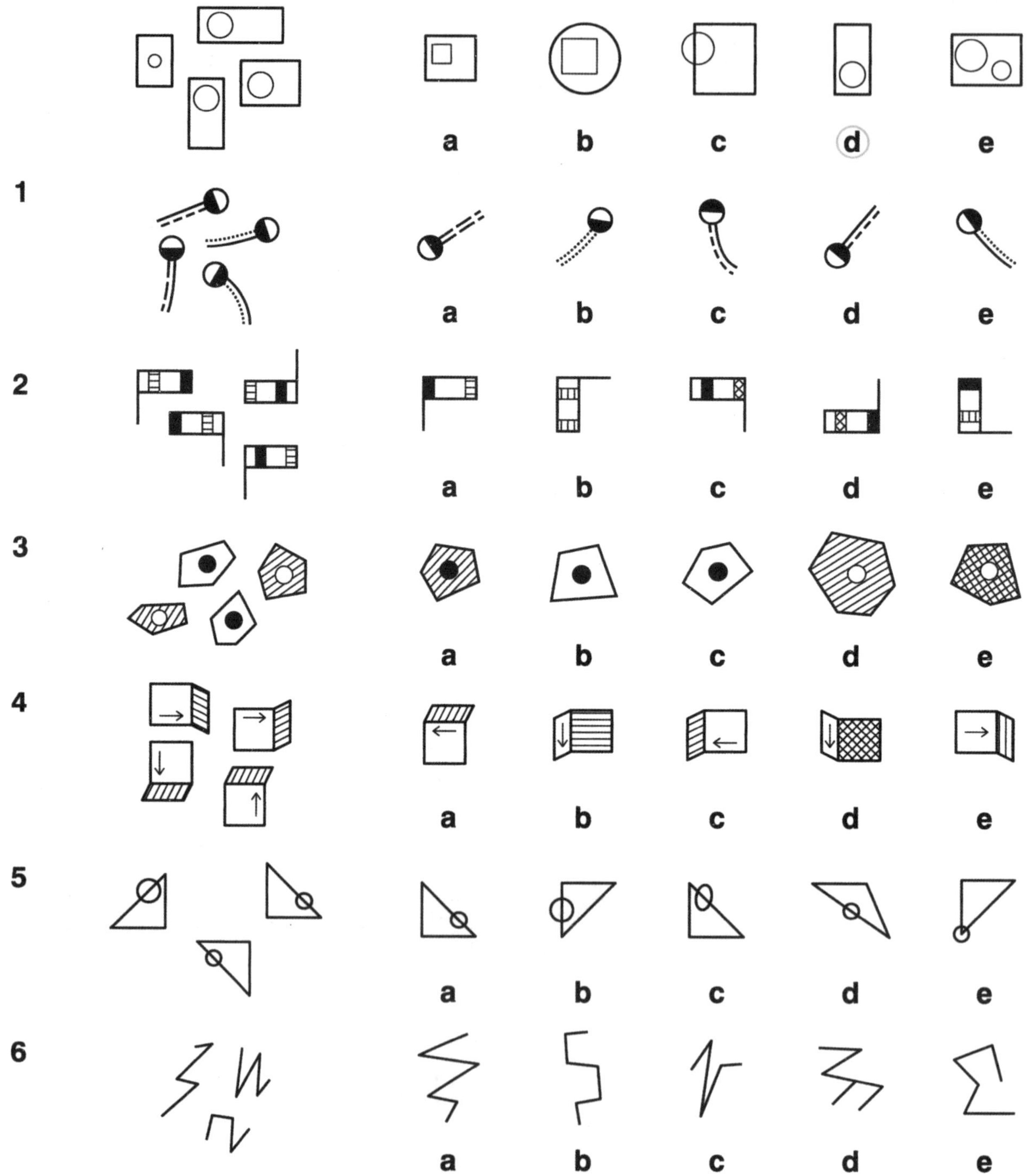

Example

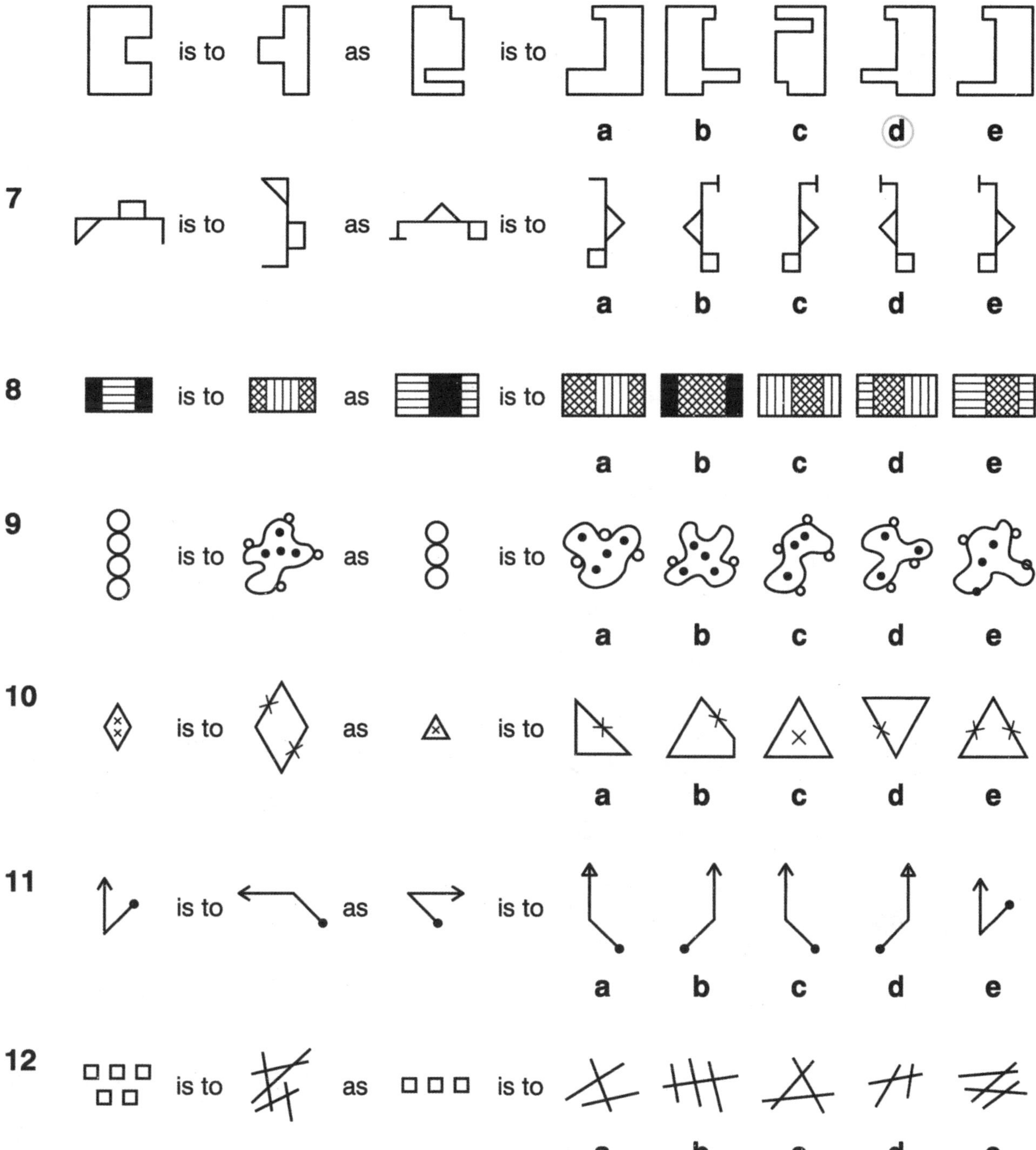

Using the given patterns and codes, work out the code that matches the last pattern. Circle the letter.

Example

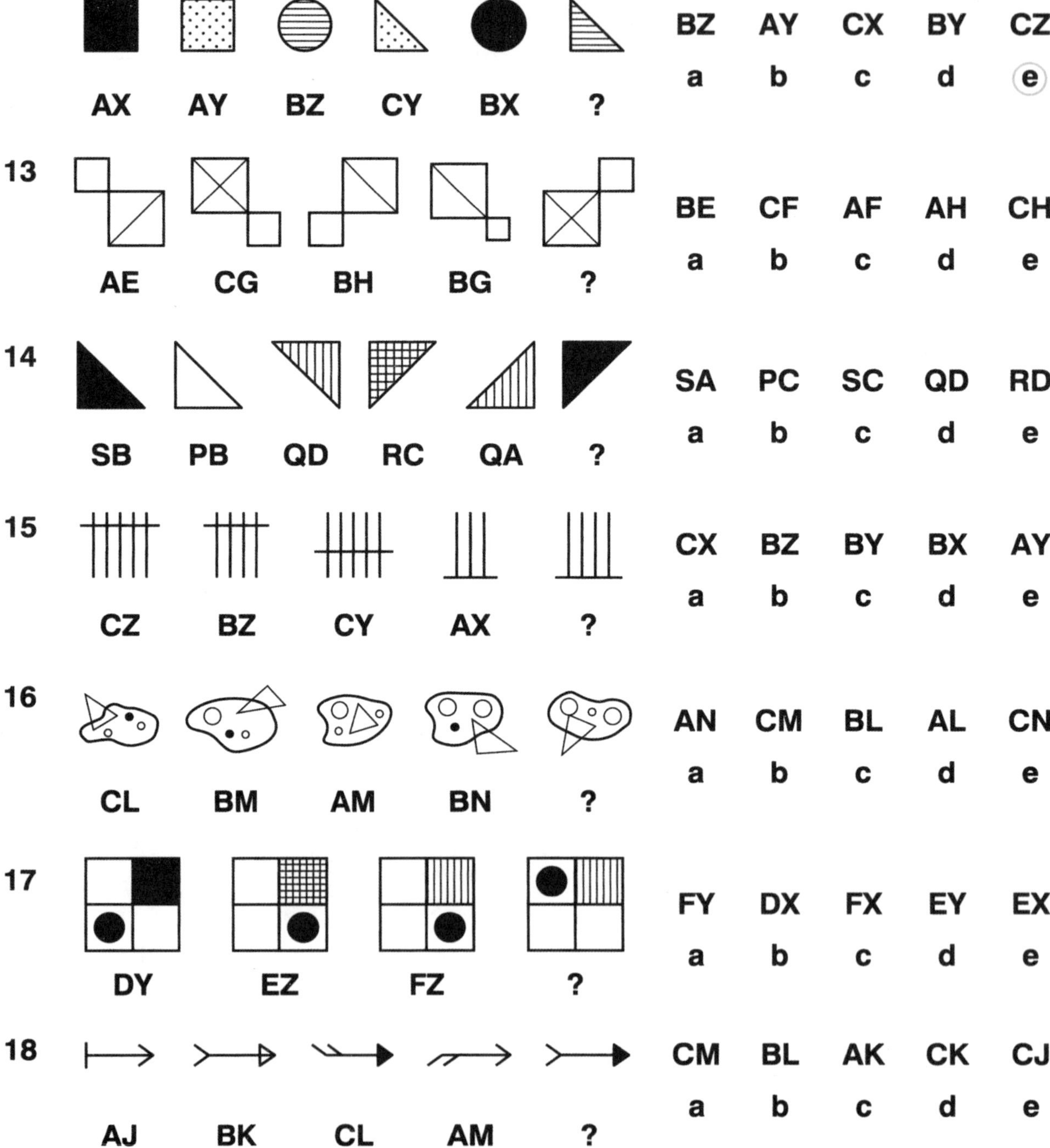

	BZ	AY	CX	BY	CZ
	a	b	c	d	(e)

13

	BE	CF	AF	AH	CH
	a	b	c	d	e

14

	SA	PC	SC	QD	RD
	a	b	c	d	e

15

	CX	BZ	BY	BX	AY
	a	b	c	d	e

16

	AN	CM	BL	AL	CN
	a	b	c	d	e

17

	FY	DX	FX	EY	EX
	a	b	c	d	e

18

	CM	BL	AK	CK	CJ
	a	b	c	d	e

Which cube could not be made from the given net? Circle the letter.

Example

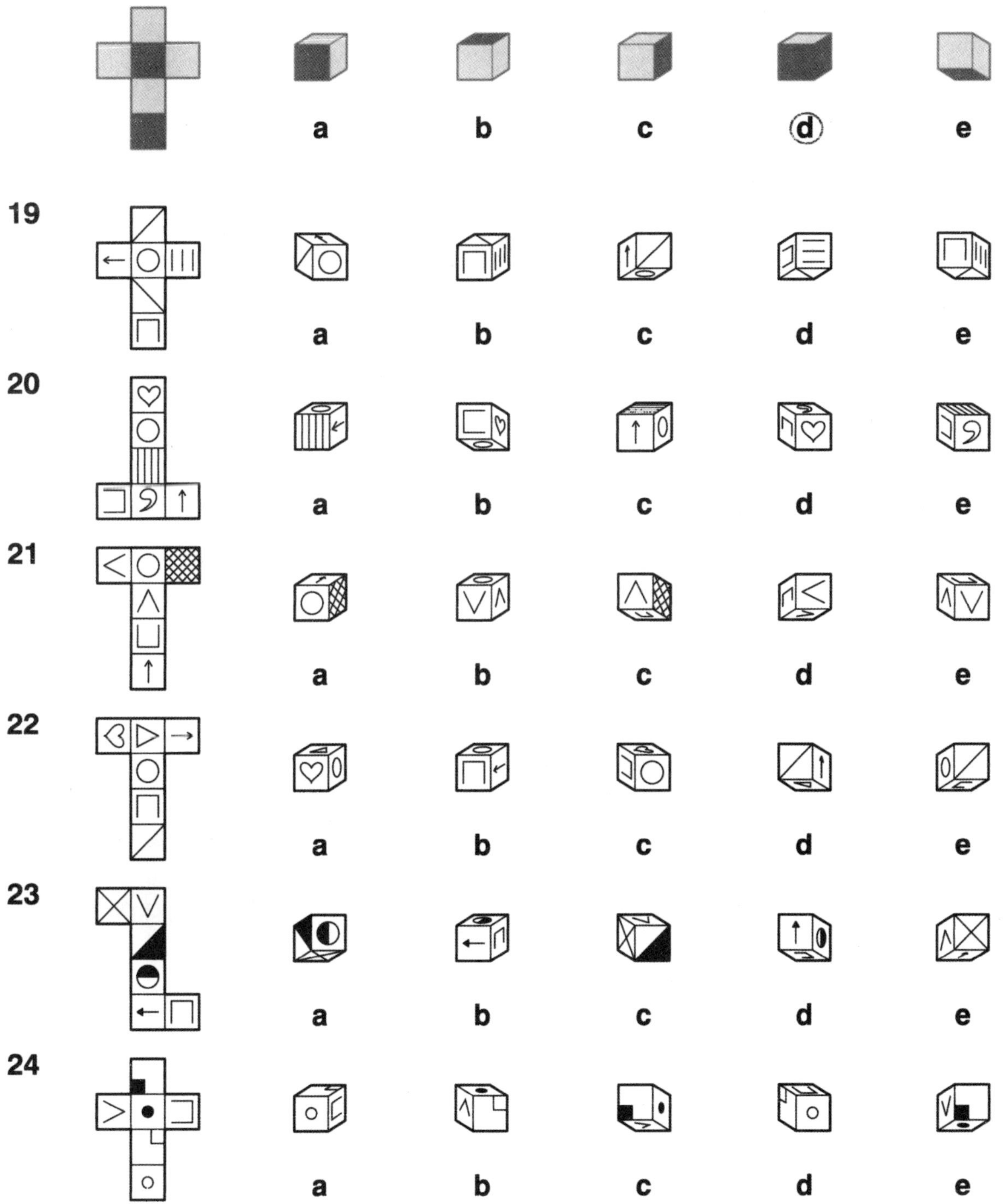

Which shape or pattern is a reflection of the shape on the left? Circle the letter.

Example

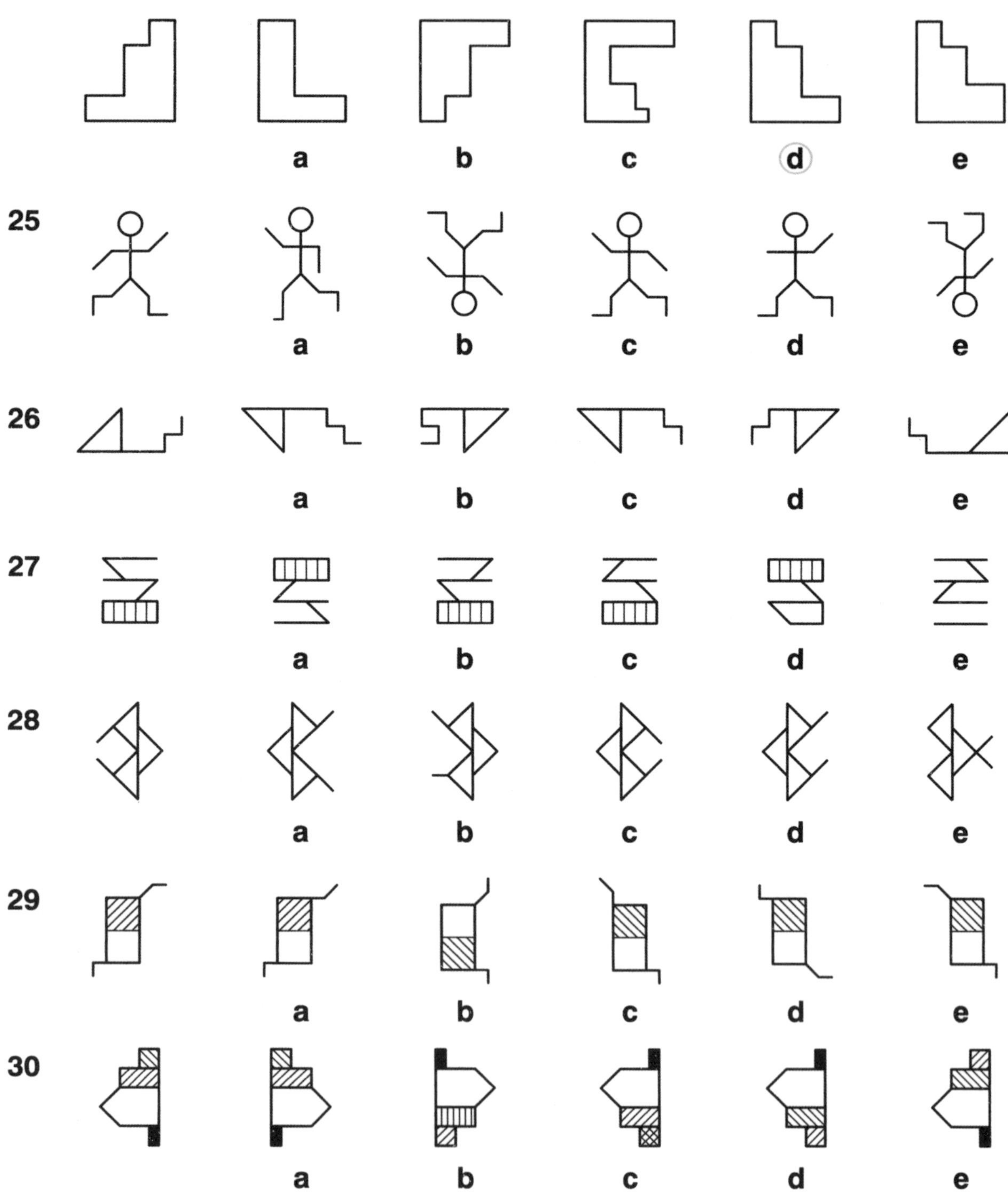

Which shape or pattern continues or completes the given sequence?
Circle the letter.

Example

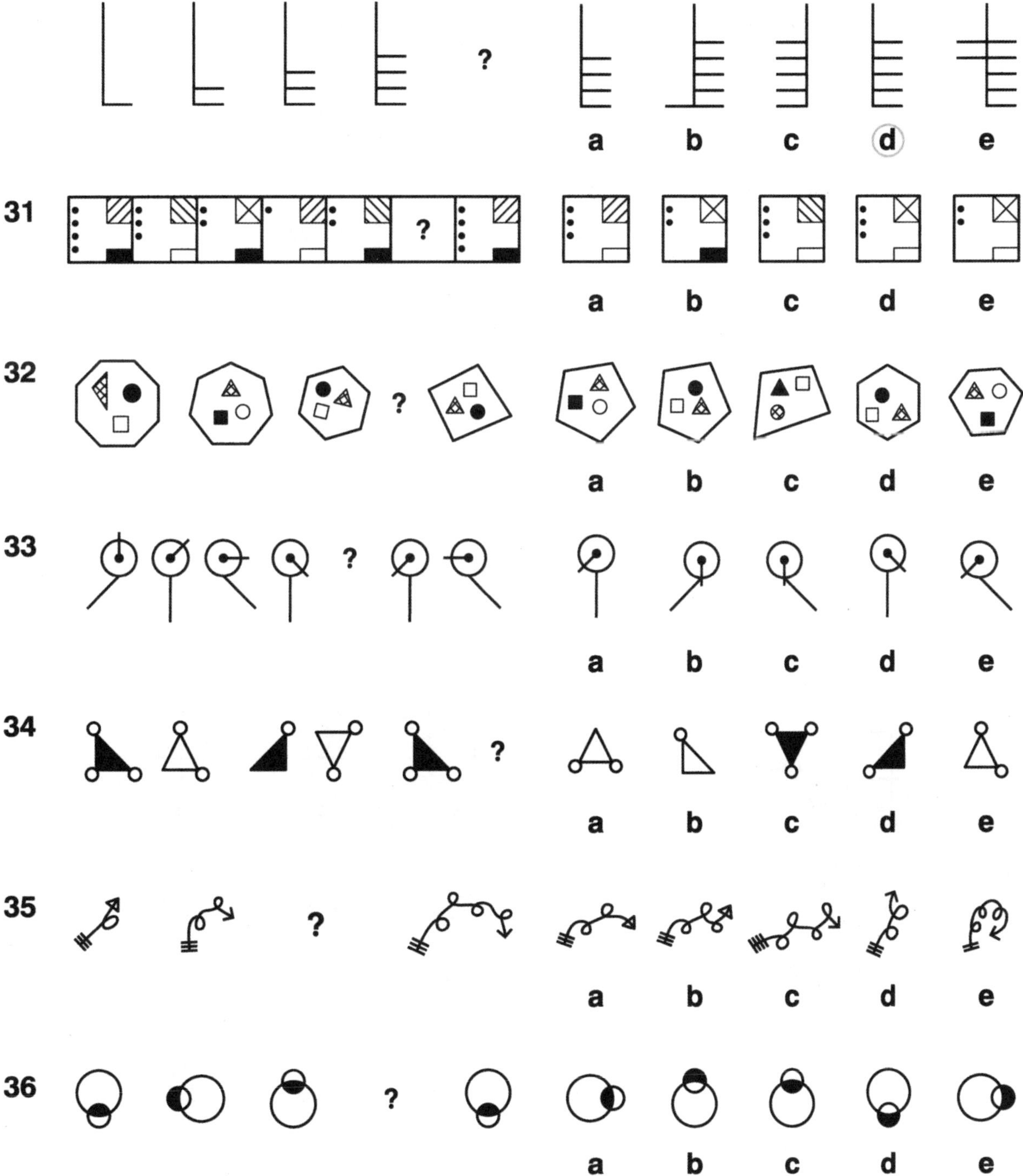

Which shape or pattern completes the grid on the left? Circle the letter.

Example

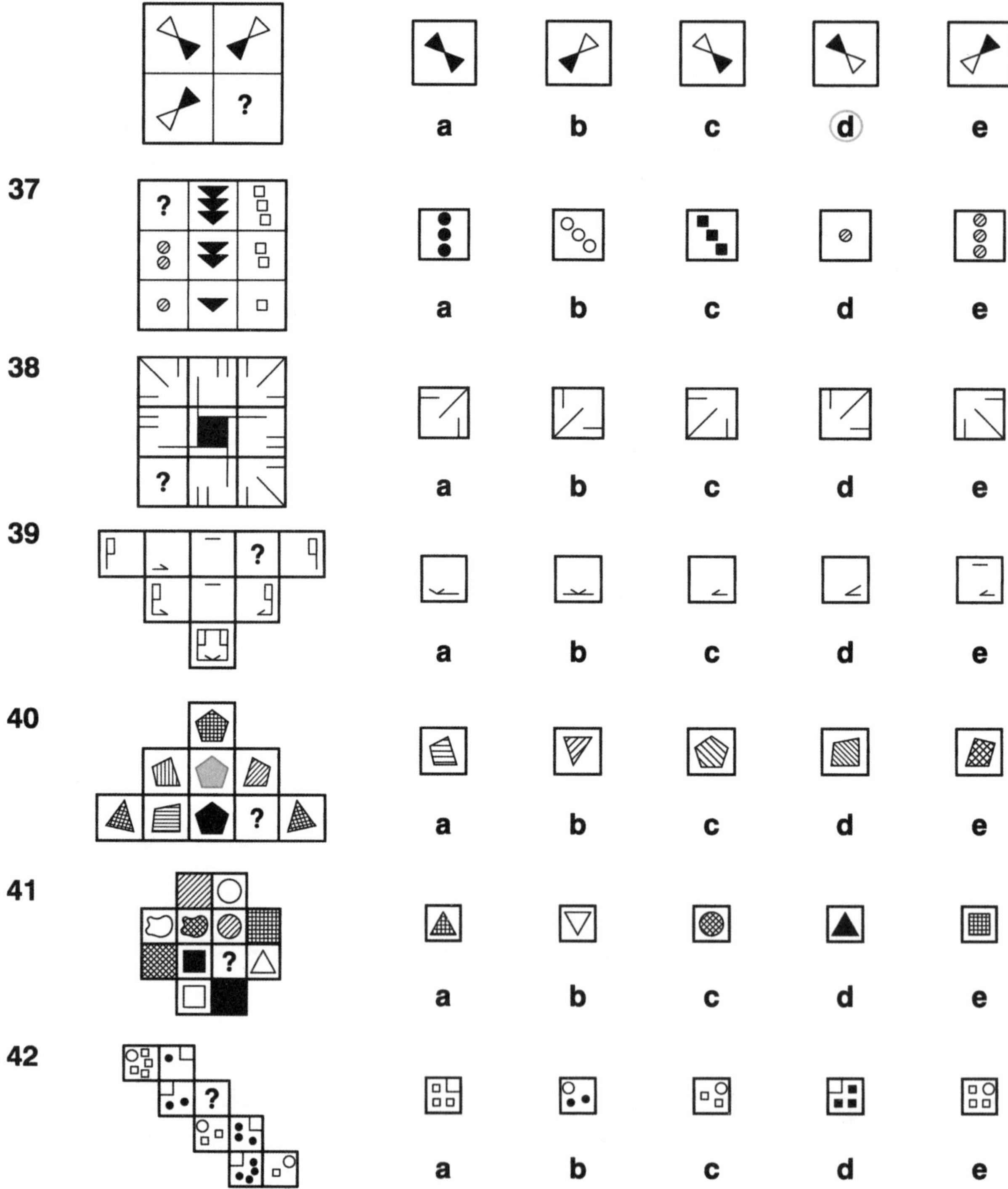

Which pattern on the right is formed by combining the two shapes on the left?
Circle the letter.

Example

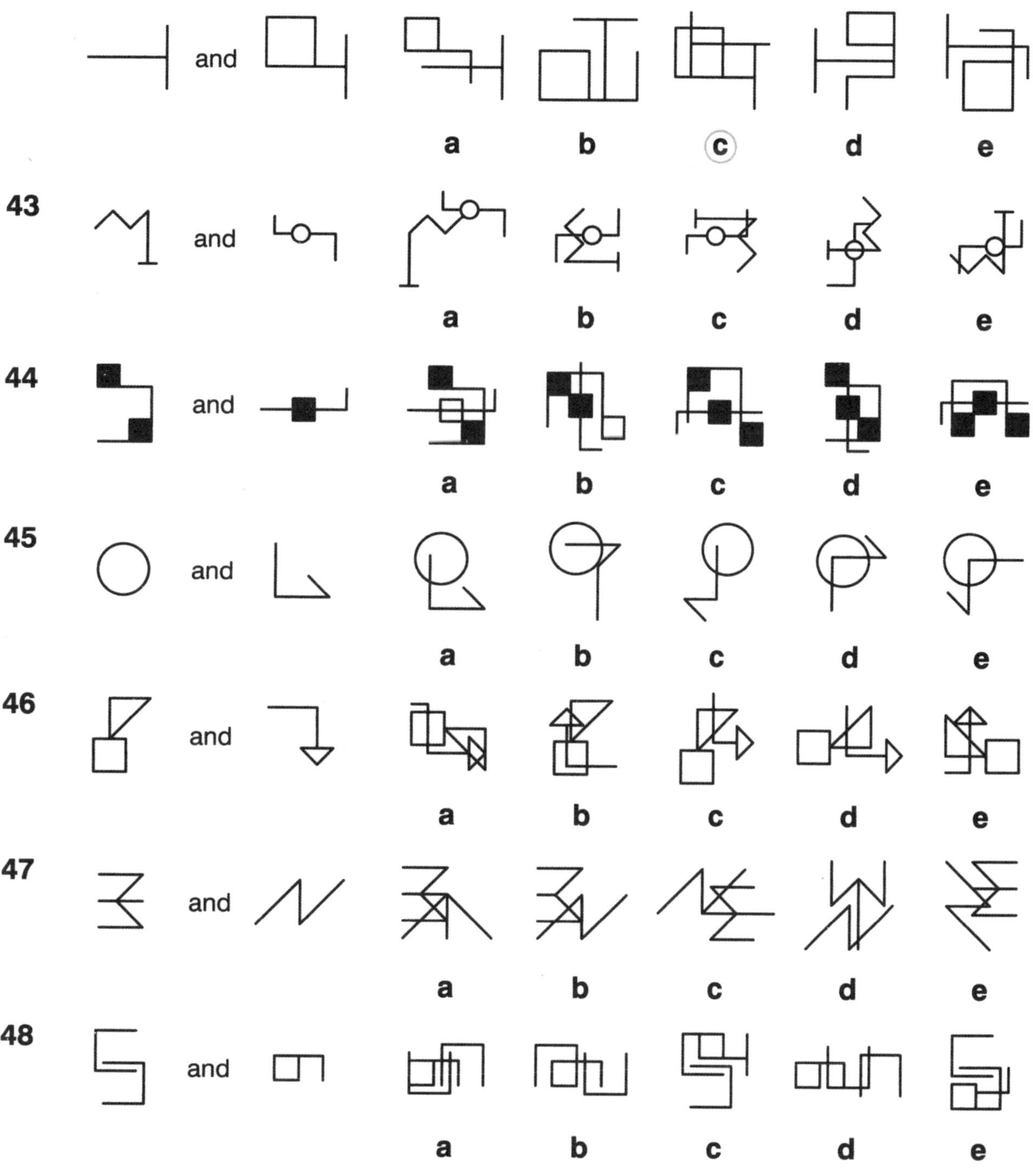